Convergent Journalism: An Introduction

Corm:
An

Stephen

ELSEVIER

AMSTERDAM • BOSTON • HEIDELBERG • LONDON
NEW YORK • OXFORD • PARIS • SAN DIEGO
SAN FRANCISCO • SINGAPORE • SYDNEY • TOKYO
Focal Press is an imprint of Elsevier

Acquisitions Editor: Amy Jollymore
Project Manager: Dawnmarie Simpson
Assistant Editor: Cara Anderson
Marketing Manager: Christine Degon
Cover Design: Cate Barr
Interior Design: Julio Esperas

Focal Press is an imprint of Elsevier
30 Corporate Drive, Suite 400, Burlington, MA 01803, USA
Linacre House, Jordan Hill, Oxford OX2 8DP, UK

Library of Congress Cataloging-in-Publication Data
Application submitted

British Library Cataloguing-in-Publication Data
A catalogue record for this book is available from the British Library.

ISBN 13: 978-0-240-807249
ISBN 10: 0-240-80724-3

For information on all Focal Press publications
visit our website at www.books.elsevier.com

05 06 07 08 09 10   10 9 8 7 6 5 4 3 2 1

Printed in the United States of America

Contents

Acknowledgments   ix

1   What Is Convergence and How Will It Affect My Life?   3
Stephen Quinn, Professor of Journalism

Fragmenting Audiences   8
Technology   9
Social and Legal Structural Factors Affecting Convergence   10
"Easy" versus "Difficult" Convergence   11
How Widespread Is Convergence?   12
Business Models and Convergence   14
Cultural Factors   15
Why Is This Book Needed?   16

2   The Multimedia Assignment Editor and Producer   21
Terry Heifetz, Managing Editor NewsLink
Indiana Converged News Service

Advantages of Each Medium   26
Covering the News in the Multimedia World   27
Covering Breaking News   30

3   Words: The Foundation Stone of Journalism   39
Vincent F. Filak, Assistant Professor of Journalism
and Adviser to Daily News

Technology and Toys Can't Save You   40
How to Write Well   41

Welcome Back, Old Friend   43
Putting It Together   44
The Editing Process   47
Conclusion   50

4 Broadcast Writing and Speaking   55

Robert A. Papper, Professor of Telecommunications

Rules for Readability   56
Rules for Understandability   58
Story Formats   62
A Closer Look   64

5 Writing for the Web   69

Wright Bryan, Former Web News Editor,
NewsLink Indiana Converged News Service

Traditional News Writing and the Web   70
Telling Your Story through Multiple Media   74
Blogs: Do-It-Yourself Journalism   75
Changing Attitudes to Fit the Web   77

6 Converged Graphics Across All Media   81

Jennifer George-Palilonis, Instructor of Journalism
and Graphics Sequence Coordinator

Information Graphics History   82
Role of the Graphics Reporter   86
One Story, Multiple Graphics   89
The Power of Information Graphics   94

7 Digital Still Photography   99

Thomas A. Price, Assistant Professor of Journalism
and Photojournalism Sequence Coordinator

The Power of the Still Photograph   99
Impact of Technology on Photographic Reporting   100
The Democratization of Photography   102
The Birth of Modern Photojournalism   104

The Digital Age   104
Picture Editing for Different Media   105
Photographers' Responsibilities for Different Media   107
Conflicting Ethical Standards among Media Outlets   109
Positive and Negative Aspects of the Multiple-Medium Photographer   110

8 Digital Video Photography   115

Tim Underhill, Production Manager,
NewsLink Indiana Converged News Service

The Professional Television Camera   115
White and Black Balancing   116
Composing Images for the Screen, Television, and Computer   117
Audio: A Sound Foundation   119
Putting It All Together to Tell a Story   121
Story Building   122
Get to Work   123

9 Editing for Moving Pictures   127

John C. Dailey, Assistant Professor of Telecommunications

A Brief Look at Nonlinear Editing Software   128
In the Field   128
Part 1: The FCP Interface   129
Part 2: The NLE Process   138
Conclusion   143

10 Multimedia Journalism: Putting It All Together   147

Stephen Quinn, Professor of Journalism

Multimedia Skills   156
The Multimedia Process   157

11 Multimedia Advertising   163

Michael Hanley, Assistant Professor of Journalism

Advertising Defined   164
A Little Bit of History   165
A New Electronic Mass Medium Is Born   166

Media Advertising: A Game of Eyeballs 168
Weaving a Web of New Media 169
Searching for Ad Revenues on the Web 170
E-Mail: The Internet Killer APP That's Getting Spammed 171
Making It Personal on the Internet 171
Staying Connected with Instant Messaging 172
Let the Games Begin 174
Blogs Move Mainstream . . . and Mobile 175
Advertising Grows as New Digital Media Evolves 176
Advertisers Evolve to Multimedia 176
Personalized Media: The Future of Advertising 178
The Consumer Has the Power 179

12 Multimedia Public Relations 185

Robert S. Pritchard, Assistant Professor of Journalism

Public Relations in the Digital Age: What's Changed and What Hasn't 186
Using Multimedia to Build Relationships 190
Using Multimedia to Communicate with the Media 193
Using Multimedia to Communicate with Employees 197
Using Multimedia to Communicate with Communities 200
Conclusion 201

13 Where Do We Go from Here? Possibilities in a Convergent Future 205

Stephen Quinn, Professor of Journalism, and
Vincent F. Filak, Assistant Professor of Journalism

"The Future" of Media 207
Changes in How We Work, Not What We Do 208
Everything Is Knowable 210

About the Authors 213
Index 219

Acknowledgments

We would like to thank the following individuals for their assistance on this project: the faculty and staff of the College of Communication, Information, and Media (CCIM) at Ball State University. With approximately 2,300 undergrads and 200 graduate students, CCIM is one of the 10 largest media colleges in the United States. Had it not been for the CCIM's cutting-edge approach to all forms of media, this book would have been incomplete in its scope and lacking in its composition. Thanks to Acting Dean Michael Holmes, Associate Dean Jacquelyn Buckrop, Journalism Chair Marilyn Weaver, and Telecommunications Chair Nancy Carlson for access to your amazing faculty members.

Special thanks go out to the authors who gave of themselves to help provide their expertise on a vast array of topics: Wright Bryan, John Dailey, Jenn George-Palilonis, Michael Hanley, Terry Heifetz, Bob Papper, Tom Price, Bob "Pritch" Pritchard, and Tim Underhill. This text is unique in the way it brings together the talents of educators and practitioners to develop a book that contributes to the new world of media work known as convergence. We were truly fortunate to be able to draw from the knowledge of so many great individuals.

Thanks to the reviewers from Focal Press, who provided us with good feedback and solid ideas. Thanks also to the staff at Focal, including our editor, Amy Eden Jollymore, and her assistant, Cara Anderson, who helped edge us along toward the finish line. Thanks also go out to Greg Hollobaugh at MSNBC.com and Don Wittekind, graphics director at the *South Florida Sun-Sentinel*, for allowing us to share your work with our audience.

Finally, we would like to thank our families for their patience and understanding as we worked to complete this task. Nothing is possible without your support.

Teenagers and young adults roam through the streets of downtown Gwangju, South Korea, on a Friday evening in early Spring 2005. (Photograph courtesy of Amanda Goehlert.)

What Is Convergence and How Will It Affect My Life?

Convergence is a revolutionary and evolutionary form of journalism that is emerging in many parts of the world. As a student graduating from a journalism program in the early 21st century, you need to know about convergence because it is likely to influence the way your career evolves. Over the course of the next decade, you probably will work in several media platforms, perhaps with different companies, but also possibly with the same company but doing varied forms of journalism. All journalists need to know how to tell stories in all media, and how to write appropriately for those media, as preparation for this new era.

What is convergence? Just as beauty is in the eye of the beholder, most definitions of convergence depend on each individual's perspective. Indeed, convergence tends to have as many definitions as the number of people who practice or study it. That's because convergence varies from country to country, and from culture to culture both within countries and individual companies. Other influential factors include laws that regulate media ownership and the power of digital technology. The type of convergence that evolves in any given company will be a product of that company's culture. As editor, John Haile introduced convergence at the *Orlando Sentinel* in 1995. "The big thing I try to emphasize with anyone looking at how to practice journalism across multiple media is the critical need to address the culture of the organization." Success depended, he said, on having journalists who could "think multiple media" and who were comfortable working across several media platforms.

Paul Horrocks, editor-in-chief of the *Manchester Evening News*, part of the Guardian Media Group in the United Kingdom, believes newspapers have to reinvent themselves to satisfy consumers eager to receive information. He argues that audiences are converged already and get information in a variety of ways. Michael Aeria, editorial manager of the Star Publications Group in Malaysia, similarly sees convergence as an opportunity for his company to reach multiple audiences. A Danish newspaper editor, Ulrik Haagerup, believes convergence has "everything to do with mindset" and how journalists see their role in society.

Larry Pryor, a professor with the Annenberg School for Communication at the University of Southern California, maintains that a definition is vital because a new idea needs a common vocabulary. "If we all have a different concept of what convergence means, we are making it difficult to progress." For this book, convergence is not about what Pryor calls "corporate conglomeration," where big companies merge because of the mutual benefits of amalgamation. Probably the best known of these was the $165 billion AOL-Time Warner merger announced in January 2000. This book is also not about the technological and sometimes utopian view of convergence that proposes that many pieces of digital equipment will converge in a single box in the living room or study.

This book discusses convergence as a form of journalism. For Pryor, convergence is what takes place in the newsroom as editorial staff members work together to produce multiple products for multiple platforms to reach a mass audience with interactive content, often on a 24/7 timescale. Professor Rich Gordon of Northwestern University has identified at least five forms of convergence in the United States, as summarized here:

❶ *Ownership convergence.* This relates to arrangements within one large media company that encourage cross-promotion and content sharing among print, online, and television platforms owned by the same company. The biggest example in the United States is the Tribune Company. President Jack Fuller said that owning television, radio, and newspapers in a single market provided a way to lower costs, increase efficiencies, and "provide higher quality news in times of economic duress"

(Gordon, 2003, p. 64). Other smaller but successful examples were the News Center in Tampa, where the *Tampa Tribune*, NBC-affiliated WFLA-TV, and TBO.com were all owned by the Media General company; and in Columbus, Ohio, where the Dispatch Media Group owned *The Columbus Dispatch*, CBS-affiliate WBNS-TV, and the 24-hour Ohio News Network plus a range of Web sites and community-focused publications.

2 *Tactical convergence.* This describes the content-sharing arrangements and partnerships that have arisen among media companies with separate ownership. The most common model is a partnership between a television station or cable channel and a newspaper where each company keeps its own revenues. Gordon noted: "In most markets, the primary motivation for—and initial results of—these partnerships seemed to be promotional" (2003, p. 65). The relationship between *Florida Today*, based in Melbourne on Florida's east coast, and WKMG-TV, headquartered in Orlando, about 70 miles away to the west, provides an example. This form of convergence has become most common in the United States. The American Press Institute publishes a convergence tracker on its Web site and it represents a useful source for details across the country. Between June and September 2004, Ball State University professors Larry Dailey, Lori Demo, and Mary Spillman surveyed editorial managers at all 1,452 daily English-language newspapers in the United States. They received 372 replies, a response rate of 25.6 percent. They reported that almost 30 percent of daily newspapers had partnerships with television stations, at various circulation levels (Saba, 2004).

3 *Structural convergence.* This form of convergence is associated with changes in newsgathering and distribution, Gordon wrote, but it is also a management process in the sense of introducing changes in work practices. An example was the *Orlando Sentinel's* decision to employ a team of multimedia producers and editors to repackage print material for television. The team rewrites print content in a form suitable for television; meanwhile, a separate Web site produces original material and also repackages content from the newspaper and television partner. They also produce focused content, such as television programs about the movies and high school sports, and arrange talkbacks between print reporters and the television partner. Talkbacks consist of a conversation between the television anchor and a specialist reporter in the field. Dailey and his colleagues reported that 29.6 percent of respondents said a reporter—usually a beat expert—appeared on a partner's broadcast to explain a story at least once a month (Saba, 2004).

4 *Information-gathering convergence.* This takes place at the reporting level and is Gordon's term for situations where media companies require reporters to have multiple skills (2003, p. 69). In some parts of the world, this represents the most controversial form of convergence as people debate whether one person can successfully produce quality content in all forms of media. Several terms have arisen to describe this phenomenon, including *platypus* or *Inspector Gadget* or *backpack* journalism. The single multimedia reporter may be an appropriate and workable option at small news events or at small market media organizations. But at a major news event where groups of mono-media reporters outnumber a single multimedia reporter, this form of reporting is not likely to produce quality. Digital technology makes the multi-skilled journalist possible, but we won't see too many Inspector Gadgets until journalists are sufficiently trained and equipped. The type of cross-platform training needed to produce these journalists has always been a problematic issue in the United States.

5 *Storytelling or presentation convergence.* Gordon said this type of convergence operates at the level of the working journalist, though it needs management support in terms of purchasing the most appropriate equipment. He predicted that new forms of storytelling would emerge from the combination of computers, portable newsgathering devices, and the interactive potential of the Web and television, as journalists learned to appreciate each medium's unique capabilities (2003, p. 70). Many journalists are pondering how to do this form of convergence. Doug Feaver, executive editor of washingtonpost.com, said his journalists were "inventing a new medium" as they worked. This form of convergence remains in the experimental or evolutionary phase in many newsrooms but we may see it emerge as more and more people graduate with advanced digital skills.

Dr. Juan Antonio Giner prefers the analogy of the circus to describe convergence. He suggested that newspaper companies in the early 21st century were experiencing what happened to the circus business half a century earlier. "The one-man circus became a one-ring family circus and the one-ring family circus became the three-ring family circus." Giner said most forms of newspaper and television convergence were more like multiple independent operations than pure collaboration. That is, different family circuses with different cultures shared the same tent, but in each ring they still were acting as a single circus. Real convergence only occurred when circuses mixed animals and people under the same tent and appointed a "three-ring master," he said. "My best advice is this: go to Ringling Brothers and Barnum & Bailey Circus and there, not at Florida newspapers, you will see the Greatest Convergence Show on Earth. They are the real integrators, not the U.S. newspapers that still are in the era of three separate rings" (Giner, 2001a).

This book will argue that convergence coverage should be driven by the significance of the news event. Larry Pryor's definition discussed earlier in the chapter noted that convergence occurred in the newsroom as staff worked to produce "multiple products for multiple platforms to reach a mass audience with interactive content, often on a 24/7 timescale." That is a fine definition. If pressed for a simpler definition, we would argue that convergence is about doing journalism and telling stories using the most appropriate media. The importance of the news event should dictate the depth and type of coverage, and influence the size of the team involved. Multimedia assignment editors will decide on the most appropriate medium for telling the story. (See Chapter 10 for examples and case studies of how this works in the real world.) A major explosion downtown may require a team of still photographers, editors, video journalists, online specialists, and reporters. A routine media conference with a business leader may need only one reporter. Kerry Northrup set up the Newsplex (the prototype multiple-media newsroom set up to explore the technologies and techniques of convergence) and was its first director (see www.newsplex.org). In 2004 he became Ifra's director of publications, responsible for all five editions of the prestigious industry journal, *newspaper techniques*. He noted that assignment editors (the people who allocated stories to reporters) were the key people in convergent journalism. That is why they are discussed so early in the book's structure.

Why is convergence emerging? Several forces, working together, render this form of journalism possible. The main factors are the

7

fragmenting of audiences, the availability of relatively cheap digital technology, and changes in social and legal structures that make cross-media ownership more possible. Media companies hope they can reach fragmented audiences through multiple media, recognizing that consumers have already embraced convergence, in the sense that they use a multitude of media. Let's look at each of these drivers.

Fragmenting Audiences

As well as being exposed to a lot more media nowadays, people are using media in multiple forms to fit everything into their busy lives. The *2004 Communications Industry Forecast* showed that in the United States, the average consumer spent 3,663 hours a year in 2003 using all forms of media. That's an average of more than 10 hours a day reading, listening, watching, and surfing for any combination of professional and personal reasons. It represented an increase of almost an hour a day since 1998. James Rutherford, executive vice president of the company that published the *2004 Communications Industry Forecast*, pointed out that consumers were using two or more media simultaneously to cope with the range of media choices and the competition for attention. "The result is a media generation consuming more information in less time than ever. Time is the most precious commodity." Analysts at Rutherford's company, Veronis Suhler Stevenson (VSS), predicted the time an average American spent with media would increase by another hour a day by 2008. *Tampa Tribune* publisher Gil Thelen has pointed out that people's information-seeking behaviors are changing and media organizations need to adapt to respond to that need. Howard Tyner, a former editor of *The Chicago Tribune* who became a senior vice president of the Tribune Company, has long maintained that the business of journalism is about "eyeballs"—getting as many people as possible to look at media products. "A media company's game is to deliver content to consumers," he said. "The newspaper is and will be for a long time the engine to gather and edit news. But it won't be enough to just deliver that information to newspaper readers. We [also] need for our news and information to go to the eyeballs of Web consumers and TV viewers and cable customers and even radio listeners, although they aren't using their eyes" (Tyner, 2004). Convergence increases an organization's chances of reaching the largest number of eyeballs.

Convergence also makes news available when people want it and in the form they want it, rather than expecting audiences to consume news when networks and newspapers make it available. Audiences have fragmented, and intermedia competition has increased. Paul Horrocks, editor-in-chief of the *Manchester Evening News* in the United Kingdom, summarized the situation this way: "We must reinvent our product to be more competitive and [to] satisfy our consumers." Convergence was the answer, he said, because it reached audiences eager to receive information in a variety of forms (Pascual, 2003, p. 34). In April 2004, John Sturm, president of the Newspaper Association of America, told the group's annual meeting that traditional "ink on paper" companies had the chance to transform themselves into more broad-based media. People were demanding instant content on what mattered to them and newspapers had to exploit technology to provide that content. "People want to consume their media where, how and when they choose," he said.

Some people in advanced societies tend to be time poor but asset rich. In some parts of the United States the battle for people's disposable time has become more vigorous than the fight for their disposable income. These people tend to demand convenience, and they are usually willing to pay for it—hence the surge in online commerce and subscription services, drive-through services, the wide range of take-out food outlets, and the boom in purchase of labor-saving devices. People grab their news in the form that is most convenient. *The Wall Street Journal*'s front-page summary column, "What's News," recognizes the needs of busy businesspeople. Brazilian editorial manager Ruth de Aquino has suggested that the concept of news is changing and becoming "more personalized, more service-oriented and less institutional" (2002, p. 3).

Technology

Almost three in four American people had Internet access at home as of early 2004. A Nielsen/NetRatings survey reported in March 2004 that about 204.3 million people, or 74.9 percent of the population, receive Internet access via telephone modems at home. This was a big jump from the 66 percent reported a year earlier. The vast bulk of businesses provided fast access at work. Broadband boosts convergence because people can quickly download bandwidth-greedy content such as multimedia. In 2003, the number of American homes with high-speed Internet service jumped somewhere between 4.3 and 8.3 million, to total 23.1 to 28.2 million households, depending on source data. Forrester Research provided the more conservative figure, while the Federal Communications Commission (FCC) reported the higher figure. Jupiter Research predicts the number of home broadband users will jump to 108 million people by 2009, almost double the 55 million the company counted in 2004 (Kerner, 2004).

In February 2004 the chairman of the New York Times Company and publisher of *The New York Times*, Arthur O. Sulzberger, Jr., told a conference at Northwestern University that convergence was "the future" for the media. He said his company had acquired companies such as the Discovery Channel to allow *Times* journalists to tell stories in print, online, and on television. "Broadband is bringing us all together," Sulzberger said. "We have to do it in papers, digitally and on TV. You can combine all three elements. News is a 24/7 operation, and if you don't have the journalistic muscles in all three [platforms], you can't succeed in broadband." Sulzberger described the process as "a hell of a challenge" (quoted in Damewood, 2004).

10

Social and Legal Structural Factors Affecting Convergence

Technological change tends to gallop ahead of legal changes because regulations take time to be implemented, while technology always appears to be moving forward. Regulation is a key factor in the emergence of convergence, in the sense of providing a framework for its evolution. Singapore provides an example of the influence of legal factors on the development of convergence. Until 2000, the country's two media giants operated a comfortable duopoly: Singapore Press Holdings (SPH) ran all print media and the Media Corporation of Singapore (MCS) ran all broadcasting. SPH published eight dailies: three English, three Chinese, one Malay, and one Tamil. MCS operated five television and 10 radio channels—the bulk of Singapore's broadcasting. Laws that allowed one company to own print and broadcast media were enacted in 2000. MCS launched *Today*, a tabloid daily. SPH announced plans to launch two television channels: an English-language channel called TV Works, and Channel U, its Chinese-language equivalent. SPH hired consultants from Reuters and the BBC to prepare its print journalists to supply content for the two channels' news and current affairs programs. A battle for audiences soon took place between Singapore's two major media groups, as each ventured in different directions down the multiple-platform path.

Early in June 2003 America's Federal Communications Commission (FCC) approved controversial changes to the rules governing media ownership. These changes have the potential to influence the spread of convergence. Rules on newspaper and television ownership have not been updated since the mid-1970s, when cable television was still an infant and the Internet almost unknown. Chairman Michael Powell and his two Republican allies won the vote 3–2 and proposed new rules, yet to be implemented, that permit media companies to own more outlets within a market. Multiple groups appealed the decision in various federal courts. These cases were consolidated and assigned by lottery to the U.S. Court of Appeals for the Third Circuit.

In terms of convergence, the proposed FCC changes ease limits on owning a newspaper and a television station in the same market in the majority of large markets, and ease restrictions on cross-ownership of radio and TV stations in the same market. Most analysts agree that if the laws change many media companies will swap properties to enable them to own a newspaper and a television station in one city, and convergence will become more common. Media General owns 26 daily newspapers and 27 television channels, mostly in the southeast of the country. Chairman and CEO J. Stewart Bryan announced his plans just before the June 2003 changes: "Any of the places where we have a newspaper, we'd like to have a TV station . . . . Any of the places we have a TV station, we'd like to have a newspaper" (Steinberg and Sorkin, 2003, C6).

"Easy" versus "Difficult" Convergence

Professor James Gentry, former dean of the William Allen White School of Journalism and Mass Communications at the University of Kansas, has proposed a continuum between the "easy" and "difficult" introduction of convergence. He inserted the quote marks around the words because "there really is no such thing as easy convergence," he said. Table 1.1 lists the two extremes of the continuum (Gentry, 2004). Most of the items on this continuum are self-explanatory. Take a look at the factors listed in Table 1.1 and see where the media you are familiar with sit on this continuum.

Table 1.1 *"Easy" versus "Difficult" Convergence*

"Easy" Convergence	"Difficult" Convergence
Central to organization's strategy	Not central; secondary or worse
Committed and focused leadership	Other leadership priorities
Culture of innovation and risk taking	"Always done it this way"
Coordinating structure	No coordinating structure
Same ownership	Different ownership
Same values	Different values
Aligned systems and processes	Systems not aligned
Cable television partnerships	Partnerships with over-the-air broadcaster
Past successes together	Previous problems or no relationship
Cultures flexible or similar	Cultures not flexible or similar
Collocated	Located some distance apart
Lack of unions	Presence of strong unions

How Widespread Is Convergence?

News organizations around the world have been embracing convergence at different speeds, often faster than in the United States. In 2001 Dr. Juan Antonio Giner, founder of the Innovation International media consulting group, wrote that 7 out of 10 newspaper executives said their reporters had formal duties in at least another medium apart from the newspaper (2001b, p. 28). Newspapers were becoming "24-hour information engines" just as broadcast organizations like CNN had become 24-hour news providers. "Media diversification is the past. Digital convergence is the present. Multimedia integration is the future," Giner wrote in the online edition of *Ideas*, the journal of the International Newspaper Marketing Association (INMA). Earl Wilkinson, INMA's executive director, noted after attending a newspaper conference in Singapore that "The major newspaper companies worldwide have accepted the multimedia, brand-oriented future for newspapers." The next year Martha Stone, at the time a senior consultant for Innovation International, wrote that in nearly every country on each continent, mono-media companies were "transforming into multi-media companies, integrating editorial side operations from print, Web and broadcast divisions." The benefits of convergence were "overwhelming," she said. Stone noted that 73 percent of the members of the World Association of Newspapers (WAN) had reported some form of convergence emerging at their companies (2002, p. 1).

Media companies in Southeast Asia and Scandinavia have embraced convergence most widely as of mid-2005. In Southeast Asia the leaders include Star Publications in Kuala Lumpur, the Malaysian capital; the Nation group in Thailand; *Joong Ang Ilbo* and the Maeil Business Group in South Korea; the Singapore Press Holdings group, which publishes the prestigious *Straits Times* newspaper; and the Ming Pao Group in Hong Kong. Scandinavian media groups are especially advanced. *Aftonbladet* and the Bonnier group are Sweden's pioneers. Norway's leader is the *Aftenposten; NordJyske* is their Danish counterpart. The Turun Sanomat Group in Finland represents one of the world's leaders in multiple-platform publishing. Editor-in-chief Ari Valjakka said the key issue in Finland was people's time: Individuals spent an average of 7.5 hours a day in media-related activities. "The division of time between all possible information channels is fierce and that's why you need to be involved in more than one medium."

In Europe, the United Kingdom's leaders are *The Financial Times*, *The Guardian*, and the BBC. In Spain, the Marca Group captures 62 percent of the daily sports market through a combination of the daily newspaper (circulation 564,000) and a huge Web site that offered plenty of multimedia content. Other Spanish leaders are *La Vanguardia*, *Recoletos*, *El Mundo*, and Grupo Correo. Giner states that the South American leaders include *Clarin* in Argentina; the Reforma Group and Televisa in Mexico; *O Globo*, the O Estado de S. Paulo Group, and RBS in Brazil; *El Universal* in Caracas; *El Caribe* in the Dominican Republic; *El Nuevo Dia* in Puerto Rico; *Telefuturo* in Paraguay; *El Tiempo* in Colombia; and *Medcom* in Panama. In 2001 just over 100 newspaper companies around the world had embraced multimedia integration. By 2004 the number had jumped to about 475.

In the United States, the pioneers have tended to be grouped in Florida: the *Tampa Tribune*, the *Orlando Sentinel*, the *Sarasota Herald-Tribune*, and *Florida Today*. Other leaders were *The Washington Post*, *The Los Angeles Times*, and *The Chicago Tribune*. API's convergence tracker showed that, as of late 2004, convergence was happening in 33 of the 48 mainland states, involving about 80 relationships. Also in 2004, Howard Finberg of the Poynter Institute calculated that about 100 of the 1,457 daily newspapers in the United States had embraced convergence. The Project for Excellence in Journalism, an institute affiliated with Columbia University's Graduate School of Journalism, published a study of the state of the American news media that year. The study identified convergence as one of eight media trends.

13

Business Models and Convergence

American media are businesses, and one of the realities of business is the need to make money to sustain the supply of content. Journalism needs advertising and advertising needs journalism, because advertising pays for good reporting just as good reporting attracts customers for advertising. As editor of the *Orlando Sentinel*, John Haile saw the potential of new media—and the dangers of media fragmentation. He recognized the importance of protecting a company's revenues, and said new media and convergence offered a way to do so. "The issue driving my actions was the threat to our ability to do great journalism. I had long believed that the soundest foundation of a free and successful press was a financially successful press. As I looked to the future, I could see how that financial base could be eroded by the proliferation of new media and the almost certain fragmentation of our audience" (2003, p. 4). Haile introduced the concept of convergence in 1995 via various arrangements, including a partnership in the fall of 1998 with Time Warner, which owned the all-news cable channel Central Florida News 13. *Sentinel* reporters and editors contributed regular news and features stories throughout the day. Later that year, Haile designed and had installed a multimedia desk in the center of the newsroom as a symbol of convergence.

In the best of all worlds, the journalism–business tension resolves itself in a balance where good journalism attracts enough advertising to sustain both the journalism and the need to make a profit. If the equation gets out of balance, such as during an economic recession or when managers get greedy, the tension becomes more magnified. If the equation is balanced, convergence can work. Convergence can appear attractive to some editorial managers and publishers who think that multi-skilled journalists should potentially be able to produce more news for the same or little more money. They reason that their organizations should be able to cut costs because of increased productivity—more multi-skilled reporting means the organization needs fewer reporters. This remains one of the most popular myths about convergence. Major opportunities do exist for cross-promotion and marketing, where each medium recommends the next in the news cycle. And it is possible to save money through shared back-end facilities such as payroll and human resources if one company introduces convergence. But convergence does not cut costs in the content-producing areas. Professor James Gentry has advised several newsrooms on convergence, and written extensively on the subject. For him the bottom line can be summarized in one sentence: "Convergence always costs more than you think it will, takes longer than you think it will, and is more difficult to do than you think it will be."

From the journalist's perspective convergence offers a chance to do better journalism by giving reporters the tools to tell stories in the most appropriate medium. Technology frees them from the limits of individual media. Some print reporters are embracing convergence because appearing on television gives them added visibility—they enjoy being recognized in public places. Convergence skills also make them more marketable. Joe Brown, a senior reporter at the *San Francisco Chronicle*, said convergence also improved both forms of writing. "Across the board there is this misunderstanding between print and broadcast journalists. They sneer at each other. But once you [a print journalist] have done it [broadcast journalism] you appreciate how difficult it is. You understand the limitations of broadcast [journalism] and the skills involved. You don't take it for granted and you also understand the limitations of the other medium. I think that convergence helps [print] reporters understand what's missing in their reporting. Print reporters who wind up doing television end up understanding what's missing in their work," Brown said.

Cultural Factors

Cultural factors can encourage or inhibit convergence. Angels will not work with people they perceive as devils. A conservative newspaper that sees itself as a paper of record will have issues partnering with a tabloid television organization. Similarly, print journalists who look down on television people, labeling them as dimwit poor spellers, are less likely to welcome broadcast people into their newsrooms. A recent study found that some print and broadcast journalists are locked in a cultural clash known as an intergroup bias dynamic. The journalists who participated in this study were more likely to rate their medium and career as being more important than that of the other group. Furthermore, both print and broadcast journalists were asked to rate a plan to create a converged newsroom. Though all participants were rating the exact same plan, the study manipulated the source of the plan to be print journalists, broadcast journalists, or a combination of the two. Both print and broadcast journalists were most negative in rating the plan when they thought it was the sole work of the other

15

group (Filak, 2004). These and other cultural issues are likely to cause problems for convergence unless they are dealt with properly.

Tensions can be reduced through tasks that show journalists' shared values. Reporters learn to trust people from other media through working with them and discovering their similarities. Managers play a vital role in pointing out that journalists share the same core values. Instructors in various institutions also are seeking ways to instill these collaborative values in their students (Birge, 2004). This early intervention should help limit the likelihood that students will start down the path of "us versus them" (Filak, 2003). Another key is training in the sense of exposure to ideas, and learning how to operate in different media. Part of the problem is the language that separates print and broadcast journalists; an editor in print is very different from a broadcast editor. Working together and sharing media experiences can help diminish the perception of difference by both groups.

Why Is This Book Needed?

In 2003 Professor Edgar Huang and a group of his graduate students at the University of South Florida released details of a national survey they conducted at universities and media organizations (daily newspapers and commercial television stations). The survey asked how journalism schools should prepare students for media convergence. The results showed that three in five of America's journalism schools had adapted their curricula or developed new courses to prepare for convergence. Camille Kraeplin and Carrie Criado of Southern Methodist University found that 85 percent of the 240 university programs they surveyed had adopted or were in the process of introducing convergence to the curriculum. Some of the changes were "fairly minor" (Kraeplin & Criado, 2002). Huang concluded that a wait-and-see strategy would disadvantage journalism schools, and suggested that schools needed to provide cross-media knowledge and experience to help students find jobs. Multidimensional news reporting over multiple platforms would be the way tomorrow's news was presented, Huang concluded. "Therefore, dealing with media convergence in college journalism education is an urgent necessity" (Huang *et al.*, 2003).

This book is based on the belief that university journalism programs need to offer convergence skills. This preparatory chapter aside, the rest of the book adopts a hands-on approach. The book is a satisfying and rare blend of academic study and practical application.

The contributors are all Ball State teachers who are well versed in the theory of convergence. Many also practice their craft with media organizations, so you will also read their thoughts and their synthesis of how the industry perceives convergence. The opinions of contributors are their own and those opinions are based on their knowledge of the working media. If at times you note variations in tone and opinion, then accept that as part of what it is like to work in the media.

The next chapter discusses the vital role of the multimedia assignment editor. These people need to appreciate the strengths of each medium so they know what reporting resources to allocate to stories. Chapter 3 focuses on what is still the most important skill for a journalist regardless of medium: the ability to write clearly. It also teaches students how to edit their own work. Chapter 4 discusses writing for broadcast and how to present one's words in an appropriate style and tone. Chapter 5 continues on the writing theme, and demonstrates how to write for the Web. It also discusses the attraction of interactivity on the Web. Chapter 6 shows the power of reporting with information graphics. This chapter discusses a storytelling approach using graphics that are appropriate for all forms of media. Chapters 7 and 8 teach students how to take digital still photographs and digital video, respectively, focusing on the storytelling functions of still and moving images. Chapter 9 shows how to edit video footage, and encourages photojournalists to shoot with the editor in mind. Chapter 10 is based on the notion that, with time, more and more "platypi" or multimedia reporters may emerge from their burrows. The most likely scenarios involve wars (embedded reporters in Iraq, for example) or isolated locations where it is not possible to send a team of reporters.

The financial aspects of convergence are not ignored. Chapter 11 considers the development of multimedia advertising, while Chapter 12 assesses the role of convergent public relations. In some ways, these aspects of communication are well ahead of journalism in their adoption of convergent methods. It also bears noting that both advertising and public relations are intertwined with journalism in the United States. Chapters that examine convergence from the perspectives of PR and advertising experts can provide a unique and important look at this process. The final chapter asks where we go from here, and offers a look into an admittedly cloudy crystal ball. Each chapter contains current examples along with exercises that students can do to practice the skills that are discussed.

17

Convergence is with us. Here is your chance to learn the skills that will make you attractive to employers in the new and exciting world of multimedia.

References

Birge, E. (2004, May). Teaching convergence—But what is it? *Quill*, 92(4), 10–13.

Dailey, L., Demo, L., & Spillman, M. (2003). *The convergence continuum: A model for studying collaboration between media newsrooms.* Paper presented at the Association for Educators in Journalism and Mass Communication conference, Kansas City, MO.

Damewood, A. (2004). "New York Times publisher shares his vision for the future of journalism." See a report of Sulzberger's February 23 Crain lecture, "Journalism at the turn of the century." Retrieved March 1, 2004, from http://www.medill.northwestern.edu/inside/2004/Sulzberger

de Aquino, R. (2002, May). *The print European landscape in the context of multimedia.* Presentation at Mudia (Multimedia in a Digital Age) in Bruges, Belgium. Retrieved March 23, 2004, from http://ecdc.info/publications/index.php

Filak, V. (2003). *Intergroup bias and convergence education: A theoretical discussion of conflict reduction between print and broadcast journalism students.* Paper presented at Expanding Convergence: Media Use in a Changing Information Environment conference, Columbia, SC.

Filak, V. (2004). Cultural convergence: Intergroup bias among journalists and its impact on convergence. *Atlantic Journal of Communication, 12*(4), 216–232.

Gentry, J. (2004, February 9). *Toward a cross-platform curriculum.* Presentation at Poynter Institute, St. Petersburg, FL. Also various e-mail conversations in 2004.

Giner, J. A. (2001a). Comments posted March 8, 2001, at http://www.inma.org

Giner, J. A. (2001b). From media companies to "information engines." In *Innovations in Newspapers 2001 World Report* (pp. 28–33). Pamplona, Spain: Innovation International.

Gordon, R. (2003). The meanings and implications of convergence. In K. Kawamoto, Ed., *Digital Journalism: Emerging Media and the Changing Horizons of Journalism* (pp. 57–73). New York: Rowman & Littlefield.

Haile, J. (2003). Creating a change culture: A case study of the *Orlando Sentinel's* transition to a multi-media company. Inside Out Media.

Huang, E., Davison, K., Davis, T., Bettendorf, E., Shreve, S., & Nair, A. (2003). *Bridging newsrooms and classrooms: Preparing the next generation of journalists for converged media.* Paper presented at the AEJMC annual conference, Kansas City.

Kerner, S. (2004). "Survey: Value-adds key to broadband revenues." Retrieved April 26, 2005, from http://www.internetnews.com/stats/article.php/3468791

Kraeplin, C., & Criado, C. (2002, November 15). Convergence journalism—a new paradigm? Presentation at Dynamics of Convergent Media, Columbia, SC.

Pascual, M. (2003, July/August). The path towards convergence becoming more clear. *newspaper techniques*, pp. 34–35.

Project for Excellence in Journalism. (2004, April). The state of the news media 2004. Retrieved May 17, 2004, from http://www.stateofthenewsmedia.org/

Saba, J. (2004, October 18). Convergence study suggests papers, TV stations not working together enough. *Presstime*. Retrieved December 21, 2004, from http://www.editorandpublisher.com/eandp/search/article_display.jsp?schema=&vnu_content_id=1000673368

Steinberg, J., & Sorkin, A. (2003, May 26). "Easier rules may not mean more newspaper-TV deals." *The New York Times*, pp. C1, C6.

Tyner, H. (2004, October 11). Telephone interview.

19

Firefighters work to control a large fire that broke out in the early-morning hours of July 10, 2004, at Omnisource on the 3700 block of Maumee Avenue in Fort Wayne, Indiana. (Photograph courtesy of Will Vragovic.)

The Multimedia Assignment Editor and Producer

Tell someone you work in the news business, and they're likely to think you're a reporter, anchor, or photographer. These may be the most visible positions in a newsroom, but many behind-the-scenes jobs are just as critical. Some of the more important jobs include the assignment editor and producer. While each position is independent, the two people who hold these jobs must carefully coordinate their roles to cover the news in a cohesive, effective way. When you add convergence to the mixture, the positions become even more challenging and more rewarding.

Assignment editors are basically the traffic cops in a newsroom. They have to make sure all stories are covered with the proper resources. Here are some of the duties of the assignment editor in a traditional TV/radio newsroom:

- Maintain futures files. These describe stories that reporters and producers will use in upcoming programs. They may be newspaper clippings, news releases, or old scripts that need updating. The aim is to ensure newsrooms cover stories that are scheduled in advance, along with follow-up stories.
- Monitor police and fire scanners.

- Make beat calls to emergency and government officials. These are typically phone calls to dispatchers or administrative assistants who can release information about spot news in the community.
- Coordinate photographers and reporters in the field. The assignment desk is the primary contact with everyone who is covering something.
- Make quick judgment calls about story coverage. Since the assignment editor knows who is covering what, he or she knows which resources are available.
- Stay in constant communication with producers about breaking news and changes.
- Build contacts with newsmakers, including politicians, emergency officials, and any source who has an intimate knowledge of a subject.

In some medium and large market newsrooms (bigger than market 100), multiple assignment editors split the duties by responsibility and time of day. Big newsrooms might have a planning editor and assignment desk assistants, or there may be daytime, night, and weekend assignment editors. However, in small newsrooms, one assignment editor often fills every role, and the assignment editor may be on call 24/7.

The producer is the architect of the newscast. In the daily coverage scheme, the assignment editor chooses what stories the station will cover and assigns the reporters, photographers, and editors to cover them. The producer decides how each story will look and sound. Here are some of a producer's duties in a traditional TV/radio newsroom:

- Decide which stories will be shown or heard in a newscast. The producer is the "gatekeeper," deciding what is shown on the news and what isn't.
- Determine what form a story will take. The story could be a short voiceover, a copy story that the anchor reads, a reporter package, or a live shot from the field.
- Build the newscast to the show's time constraints, and communicate those guidelines to reporters. The producer tells the reporters how long their stories should be.
- Track progress of all reporters, photographers, and editors working on a story.

- Communicate with anchors who present the news. The producer speaks to anchors via their earpieces.
- Write and copyedit scripts. This is especially true for voiceover and copy stories and national/international stories that appear in a newscast.
- Monitor news wires, such as Associated Press, for developing stories.
- Time the show while it is airing live. The producer may have to add or drop stories, depending on how the show is timing out.
- Interact with the technical crews, especially the director. The director is the main technical person who oversees the staff that puts the newscast on the air.
- Order or build graphics needed to enhance news stories. These could be full-screen graphics or over-the-shoulder anchor graphics.
- Write headlines and teases used throughout the newscast. These are the devices used to capture and keep audience interest in the newscast.

The number of producers and their roles also depend on the market size. In the smallest markets, one person may produce multiple news-casts per day. In larger markets, multiple producers may work on one newscast. In some places, one person may act as both the producer and the assignment editor.

The roles of both the producer and assignment editor become much more complicated in a multimedia or converged newsroom. The two people must now think about more than what the stories are and how they'll be covered for a newscast. Now, they must determine the best ways to cover the story for print, broadcast, and online platforms.

There is also a fundamental difference in how newspapers are struc-tured, compared to broadcast media. In general, a newspaper covers much more news than the broadcast media, because a newspaper has much more space to fill. The words in a typical half-hour program would fill about one broadsheet page. Few newspapers have a central assignment desk. There are multiple page editors, copyeditors, and photo editors.

Another key difference between each medium is the deadline. TV and radio have several deadlines throughout the day depending on when newscasts are scheduled. Newspapers have a set deadline, usually several hours before the presses have to roll. The Web, however, has no deadline. It needs to be updated constantly.

In a fully converged newsroom, one assignment desk would oversee all news coverage and content. However, if you ask 100 people to define convergence, you'll get 100 different answers. Some see it strictly as promotion between independent newspapers and television stations and Web sites. Others see convergence as one giant newsroom, where reporters move freely from one medium to the other. Lori Demo, Larry Dailey, and Mary Spillman (2003) from Ball State University have come up with the idea of a "convergence continuum." They define the levels of convergence and what each one means, as shown in Figure 2.1.

- Cross-promotion is the process of using words and/or visual elements to promote content produced by the partner and appearing in the partner's medium (e.g., when a newscaster urges the viewers to read a story appearing in the newspaper or the newspaper publishes the logo of the television partner).

24

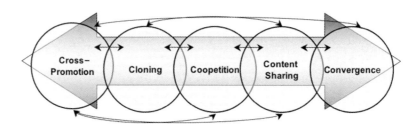

Figure 2.1 *The convergence continuum.*

- Cloning is the unedited display of a partner's product (e.g., content from a newspaper or newscast is republished on the partner's Web site or jointly operated Web portal).
- Coopetition is the point at which partners cooperate by sharing information on selected stories, but still compete and produce original content (e.g., when a newspaper reporter appears on a newscast as an expert to discuss a story or a broadcaster allows a print photographer to ride on the station helicopter to cover breaking news).
- Content sharing exists when the partners meet regularly to exchange ideas and jointly develop special projects (e.g., election coverage or investigative work).

- Convergence is the level at which partners have a shared assignment/editor's desk and the story is developed by team members who use the strengths of each medium to best tell the story.

At the left end of the continuum shown in Figure 2.1 is the *cross-promotion* level in which the least amount of cooperation and interaction occurs among members of the different news organizations. At this level, the media outlets promote the content of their partners through the use of words or visual elements. A newspaper, for example, might place a television station's logo within an article, or a television news anchor might direct viewers to the newspaper or a common Web site for more information on a story. The outlets do not work together to produce content.

To the right of cross-promotion is *cloning*, a practice in which one partner republishes the other partner's product with little editing (e.g., content from a newspaper is displayed on a TV partner's Web site or jointly owned Web portal). News outlets at the cloning level do not discuss their newsgathering plans and share content only after a story has been completed.

In the center of the continuum is *coopetition*, the stage at which news outlets both cooperate and compete. At this level, the staff members of separate media outlets promote and share information about some stories on which they are working. One entity also might produce some content for its partner, but at this level, years of competition and cultural differences combine to create mutual distrust that limits the degree of cooperation and interaction. For example, a newspaper reporter might appear as an expert or commentator on a television station's newscast to discuss a current issue, but the two staffs are careful not to divulge any information that might be exclusive to their news products.

The fourth stop on the model is *content sharing*, the level at which a media outlet regularly (but not always) shares information gathered by its cross-media partner and publishes it after it has been repackaged by the organization's staff members. The partners also might share news budgets or attend the other partner's planning sessions. Collaboration on a special, investigative, or enterprise piece is possible. In general, however, the news organizations produce their own stories without helping each other.

25

At the right end of the model is *full convergence*, the stage in which the partners cooperate in both gathering and disseminating the news. Their common goal is to use the strengths of the different media to tell the story in the most effective way. Under full convergence, hybrid teams of journalists from the partnering organizations work together to plan, report, and produce a story, deciding along the way which parts of the story are told most effectively in print, broadcast, and digital forms. The teams gather and produce content for specific projects and then disband. New teams form as additional projects present themselves.

Advantages of Each Medium

Producers and assignment editors can no longer think of stories for one medium exclusively. They need to determine the best ways to tell a story. Here's a quick look at the advantages of the media that these individuals have at their disposal:

- *Print—portable and permanent.* You can take it with you. Print allows reporters to go into great detail with both text and graphics because the space exists. If readers miss the details the first time, they can go back again and again. There can also be multiple stories taking various angles on the same topic. Finally, from an archival perspective, the permanency of newspapers provides readers with a historical document and record of the day. But newspapers are not perfect: Space is limited, it needs to be delivered, and content is static. Once a newspaper has been published, you cannot update it, so people often read news that's already a day or two old.
- *Television and radio—immediate and emotional.* News can be brought to viewers and listeners live as it happens. When reported well, audio and video can help bring viewers a lot of information in a little bit of time. People feel like they witness the news when they can see and hear it. Radio and TV have weaknesses, though. They are passive, so it's easy to miss information when you get distracted. Unless you're recording the news, once it's over, it's gone. Time limits also limit the number of stories covered and the amount of time devoted to each one.

- *Online—the best of both worlds?* Online journalism offers the immediacy of TV and radio and the space to bring people the same amount of detail as in print publications. It's easy to use, and it's interactive. You can choose how much information you want and how you use it. Unfortunately, it takes a lot of people to put together the audio, video, photo galleries, polls, and games needed to attract and retain an audience, so it's too expensive for many media outlets to do well.

Covering the News in the Multimedia World

Early ideas of convergence focused on the "super reporter," a reporter who could cover a story with a camera, notepad, and tape recorder for every medium. In some cases, this is possible, but there are only so many hours in a day. One staff member trying to report for radio, TV, print, and the Internet is likely to run into problems when trying to tell his or her stories. The more work reporters have to do, the more likely they will be to miss deadline. It is also likely that reporters who are forced to churn out stories for each medium will repeat themselves across the media platforms. This limits the storytelling in all the media and does not take full advantage of the nuances of each format. Critics of convergence have often argued that this "jack of all trades, master of none" approach would make for worse journalism. While there are examples of individuals who have done well as "backpack" journalists, the goal of this chapter is to outline the ways in which journalists with varied backgrounds can produce separate stories that take advantage of each medium's strong points.

Most newsrooms have daily editorial meetings to decide which stories to cover. The assignment editor often runs the meeting, with input from producers, reporters, photographers, and editors. At the meeting, the assignment editor decides who is covering what story. In a converged newsroom, the outcome also has to include questions such as these: Who will cover the story for which medium, what equipment is needed, and what deadlines need to be set?

Here's an example: At the morning meeting, the assignment desk mentions the 7 p.m. city council meeting. The council will vote on a controversial superstore to be built in the city. Angry residents will be there who don't want it in their backyards. The city council says that this is a depressed area of the city and that the city is willing to help pay for the store to spur economic development. This is a planned news event, so before just sending a crew to cover the story for each medium, you must ask the questions just mentioned.

First, decide how best to cover the meeting for each medium. For all media, don't forget the basics. Get multiple sides of the story by working with multiple sources. One-sided stories with one source are not acceptable. Continue to answer who, what, where, when, why, and how, along with the "so what" (i.e., is the story worth doing?). The producer (or producers) will work with the assignment editor and other staff members to decide the best way to tell the story. Here is just one way of telling the story.

- *Print: Cover the meeting in detail.* Don't forget specifics of who speaks (both residents and officials), what they say, and the votes for and against the store proposal. Show a diagram of the store's location. Talk to residents and get photos from people who live near similar stores in similar cities. Compare and contrast them. Get specific financial information about what the superstore will provide for the community and city's tax base. We easily have one main story and two or three sidebar stories here. They can be gathered at the city council meeting and over the phone. Pictures, maps, and diagrams can be taken and e-mailed to the newsroom.
- *Radio: Cover the meeting in general terms.* Here, you want to focus on the sound of council and neighbors interacting. The talk should be interesting and emotional. Remember, the best sound bites and actualities are for emotion, not information. State the facts. You don't have time to go into detail about what happened. Stick with the basics. You can direct listeners to the print or online sources for more detail. Most of the story can be gathered at the meeting. However, there may be some good natural sound opportunities in the area where the store will be built, for example, sounds of traffic and nature. Radio reporters usually cut several versions of the same story, each with a slightly different focus.
- *TV: The meeting is not the story for television.* Meetings make bad TV. Here you need to focus on the neighborhood. You'll want to show where the store would be built. Talk to neighbors, developers, and the city council before the meeting. Show what comparable stores look like and artist drawings of what this store will look like. Don't miss the meeting since you'll need to

know the outcome and there may be a few good audio and video opportunities.

- *Web: Once again, this is where most of the opportunities lie.* The first thought is to include all of the other stories on the Web site. You can always upload to your Web site a PDF of the day's newspaper article, the audio file from the radio broadcast, and the video package from the television station. This will give your audience a chance to catch up with what it might have missed. That's a good start, but many people have already gotten those stories from the newspaper, radio, or TV, so the Web must do more than repeat what other media have stated. The Web provides ways for readers to interact with a story, so give them that opportunity. Include an interactive view of what the store will look like. Add a 360-degree view of how the store will look from peoples' yards. Use extensive interviews with residents and council members about why they do or don't want the store nearby. Show a slide show of what a comparable store looks like. Maybe even throw in an exercise in which people can try designing the perfect layout. Add a poll, which asks users to cast their vote on the issue.

This is a lot of story, so how do you allocate resources? The assignment editor has to determine that, depending on who is available. First, decide where you need people:

- At the meeting
- In the neighborhood
- In the newsroom researching similar stores and cities
- In the newsroom making graphics and interactive graphics

Chances are that the "super reporter" will not be able to cover all angles of this story. So here are some examples of what you can do. There is no right or wrong answer.

Crew 1 (two people) talks with people to get several sides of the story before the meeting using a video camera and a still camera. One person gathers the information and the other gathers the multimedia. Stills can be used in print. The same or similar stills can feed the 360-degree tour and provide the photo gallery for the Web. TV uses the video. Radio can use the video camera audio for the sound. At the newsroom, the video and stills should immediately be ingested into a server for everyone to use.

Crew 2 (three people) covers the meeting. This crew also has a video camera and still camera. At the meeting, one person can gather the information for all the media. The other person gathers the sound for radio using a video camera and the stills. Because of tight deadlines, two reporters will probably be needed. One can work on Web and print materials, the other on radio and television.

While these are the only two crews in the field, people back in the newsroom will need to be working on the graphics, Web design, and infrastructure and building story elements. In realistic terms, it will probably take at least 8 to 10 people to cover this story for all media.

Covering Breaking News

Breaking news requires a different way of thinking. In this situation, the "super reporter" idea works better. Armed with a cell phone and video camera, one person (or a two-person crew) could cover this for all media. A cell phone camera doesn't take print-quality pictures, but the quality is suitable for the Web in a breaking news situation—and they're instant. The technology has improved so that you can take still frames from video that can be high quality for the Web or print purposes.

So one person can take and transmit cell phone photos for the Web, call the information to a writer in the newsroom for TV cut-ins (where the cell phone pictures could also be used) and a brief for the newspaper, and call in a breaking news radio spot. For later coverage on the same story, the assignment editor and producer may decide to allot more resources to cover the story better for each medium. Examples of good work are shown in Figures 2.2 and 2.3. Notice the rich additional content of Figure 2.2. Coverage was worked out between print, broadcast, and Web newsrooms before the story was covered. This provided the most complete coverage possible, without last-minute glitches.

In Figure 2.3, one medium's newsroom got the tip about the story, but separate newsrooms then shared information. Because of the loose deadline schedule, the reporter had the chance to write the story for several media.

NEWSLINK n|i INDIANA

go➡

HOME NEWS ELECTION 2004 YOUR NEWS CALENDAR WEATHER

Woman announced as next BSU president

By: Jon Seidel
Reporter, Ball State Daily News
Published: 05/11/2004, 17:12:25
Last Updated: 05/12/2004, 14:15:54

MUNCIE, Ind. (NLI) - Jo Ann Gora was introduced as the 13th president of Ball State University by Board of Trustees President Thomas DeWeese on Tuesday during a news conference at the BSU Alumni Center. She is the first woman to hold the post.

Gora is currently the chancellor of the University of Massachusetts Boston (UMB). She has presided over the 13,000-student commuter campus in Massachusetts for three years. During that time state funding for the school was cut by $29.4 million.

"Now it is time for me to understand the university from your perspective, based on your experience and unique expertise," Gora said.

The new president downplayed her gender, despite the fact that no public university in the state of Indiana has been led by a female president.

"It's not significant," Gora said. "Hopefully that's not what will be the most important part about me."

Gora will take office August 9. She gave no definite indication of how long she plans on staying at Ball State, but said she does not plan on leaving anytime soon.

"I hope to be at Ball State as long as you'll have me," Gora said.

Gora also plans to acknowledge last year's deaths of students Michael McKinney and Karl Harford. McKinney was shot in November by a University Police officer during an altercation, and Harford was shot in March after leaving an off-campus house party.

"I would like to visit the families of the two students," Gora said.

Most Boston faculty give her credit for the way she handled the situation.

"She managed to preserve the academic integrity of the institution in the face of the largest cuts in the United States," Steven Schwartz, chairman of the psychology department at Umass Boston, said. Schwartz also represents the faculty of UMB to the Board of Trustees at the University of Massachusetts.

Schwartz described Gora as a strong, decisive leader who created a strategic plan for UMB that not only detailed what must be done to realize her vision for the campus, but also who

*Before becoming chancellor of UMB, Gora was the provost and vice president for Academic Affairs at Old Dominion University in Norfolk, Va. Before that she served as the dean of the College of Arts and Sciences and provost of the Madison campus at Fairleigh Dickinson University. She holds master's and doctoral degrees in sociology from Rutgers University. She received her bachelor's degree from Vassar College. (Photo from Umass Boston Web site)

MULTIMEDIA

Video: Jo Ann Gora spoke briefly after being introduced on Tuesday as Ball State's next president. NewsLink Indiana was there to record the three minute speech in which Gora said she wanted to hear from the entire BSU community. (NLI/Tim Underhill)

RELATED STORIES

BSU's David Bahlmann speaks on Gora hiring
BSU's Marilyn Buck speaks on Gora hiring

RELATED SITES

The Ball State Daily News: For More Coverage of BSU
Bio: Jo Ann Gora
University of Massachusetts Boston
Ball State University

TOOLS

📧 E-mail This Story

🖨 Printer Friendly

Figure 2.2 *The announcement of Jo Ann Gora as the president of Ball State University was a heavily anticipated event in Muncie, Indiana. NewsLink and the Ball State Daily News decided to break the story on the Web. A more in-depth look at the event and its ramifications followed in the next issue of the Daily News.*

would do what, and when.

"She was very forceful," Schwartz said.

However, those same qualities helped her earn some critics at the university. Ann Withorn, a professor of social policy at Umass Boston, said she and other faculty were critical of appointments that Gora made within the university. After hiring a popular faculty member to serve as acting provost, Withorn said, Gora removed him in favor of an outsider. The move upset many faculty.

"What she needs is insiders that are really connected to the communities," Withorn said.

But Withorn conceded that Gora struggled with many problems that were not her own. Withorn said Gora is a smart administrator who does her homework.

"Some administrators are total cardboard characters," Withorn said. "She's not that."

Schwartz emphasized Gora's ability to prepare, describing a situation where she arrived at a meeting full of people she had not met, but knew everything she needed to about them.

"You give her a memo to read before you go meet with her, she's read it and knows it," Schwartz said.

Marilyn Buck, a member of the search committee that identified Gora, said she had a similar experience when Gora first met with the committee.

"She walked around and introduced herself to each person that was there," Buck said. "She also knew what each person's responsibilities were and why they were on the committee."

Joe Losco, professor of political science at Ball State and a vocal critic of the process used to hire Gora, said he was pleased with her selection.

"I think she's an excellent choice and one that shows that she probably would have been selected by an open process," Losco said. "She comes very highly recommended by her faculty."

Losco and other faculty criticized Ball State's Board of Trustees as the search began because of the private nature of both the selection of the search committee and the selection of the final candidates. A confidentiality agreement entered into by members of the Board and the search committee meant that the name of no candidate, other than the final choice, would be made public.

Tom DeWeese, chairman of the Board, said confidentiality is the only way to attract top-level candidates. However, Gora's candidacy for the presidency of Lewis and Clark College in Portland, Ore. became public last month. She withdrew from the search at the end of April.

Either way, Schwartz said Ball State has obtained a strong leader.

"It's hard to imagine they would hire her if they wanted a yes-man kind of thing," Schwartz said. "She's far from that."

Figure 2.2 *Cont'd.*

NEWSLINK n|i INDIANA

HOME | NEWS | ELECTION 2004 | YOUR NEWS | CALENDAR | WEATHER

go➡

University employee accused of punching student

By: Andy Marquis
Staff Reporter
Published: 07/13/2004, 20:51:30
Last Updated: 07/14/2004, 19:04:46

MUNCIE, Ind. (NLI) - There is reaction on the Ball State campus after formal charges were filed Tuesday against a university employee allegedly involved in a road rage incident with a student.

According to the police report, on June 24, BSU employee Thomas Donovan rear-ended Ball State student Kyra Moore at the intersection of Bethel Avenue and Clara Lane near McGalliard Road.

Detective Nathan Sloan of Muncie Police said things escalated from there.

"The way I understand it, it was a slight rear end, and then the road rage ensued from there," Sloan said.

Four witnesses and Moore said that Moore then got out of her car to exchange insurance and license information. Donovan did not wish to report the incident to police. Moore proceeded to get his license plate number.

Donovan told police that Moore physically abused him. But all of the witnesses and Moore say that Donovan tried to use Moore's keys to move her car himself.

When she tried to stop him, he got out of the car with her keys. As she tried to get them back, Donovan punched her in the eye.

▼Thomas Donovan's mug shot from his arrest, days after a June 24 confrontation with Ball State student Kyra Moore. (From Delaware County Sheriff)

MULTIMEDIA

Video: An extended edit of NewsLink's interview with Muncie Police Detective Nathan Sloan. (NLI)

Video: An extended edit of NewsLink's interview with Ball State student Kyra Moore. (NLI/Andy Marquis)

RELATED SITES

Ball State University
Muncie Police Department

TOOLS

E-mail This Story

Printer Friendly

Again according to witnesses and Moore, Donovan moved back toward his car. Moore called 911 at this point while still trying to get her keys back. Witnesses said that Donovan tried to wrestle the phone away from Moore to prevent the call but did not gain possession of it.

"I had it (the cell phone) gripped in my hands and he couldn't get it away and that's when he hit me the second time in the same spot on my right cheekbone," Moore said. "By that time, I just stepped back on the concrete median and let him take my car keys."

In Moore's account, she then watched as Donovan took off in his car -- still in possession of her keys.

Police said Donovan was arrested on the Ball State campus several days later by a Muncie Police officer, with a BSU Police officer assisting. He made bail after several hours and has returned to work.

Donovan is employed as a programmer/analyst in the Office of the Vice President of Student Affairs and Enrollment Management. He faces two Class D felonies for theft and obstruction of justice and two Class A misdemeanors for battery and interference with reporting a crime.

Ball State's Vice President of Student Affairs Douglas McConkey said he would "have to let the local system determine the facts, and then take action when that is appropriate."

Figure 2.3 *The arrest of Thomas Donovan provided an opportunity for a reporter to work across several media platforms. Andrew Marquis wrote print, broadcast, and online stories that detailed an incident in which a university employee assaulted a student after a traffic accident.*

University Communications Executive Director Heather Shupp says the university is maintaining a wait and see attitude.

"What the University's obligation to do is assess whether there is a threat, take the appropriate actions and then we need to let the justice system run its course," she said. "Everyone has rights so that those rights can be protected."

As part of its recent "Police Yourself" campaign, the university has made it clear that it will hold students responsible for their actions on and off campus, as noted in a March letter to parents from Acting President Beverley Pitts.

Pitts wrote, "We also announced that students arrested or cited by Muncie police would be referred to the Dean of Students Office to follow the same disciplinary process as students arrested or cited by our own police. By taking this step, we made our message to students very clear: we expect appropriate and lawful behavior both on and off campus, and violations of those expectations will have a direct impact on your standing with the university."

It is not clear from university statements if BSU holds its employees to similar standards.

Some students, such as senior Sarah Kriech, think employees should be held to the same standards as students.

"I mean if we're policing ourselves, they should definitely have to," she said.

Even if Donovan is convicted, there is no guarantee the university will take action. "There is no policy that says you may not work at the university if you are convicted of a crime," Shupp said.

Donovan has been employed at Ball State since March 29th of this year and has no prior disciplinary problems.

Moore told NewsLink Indiana that she is now concerned for her safety on campus because Donovan is still working at the school.

"There was no connection to her status as a student or his status as an employee [during the altercation]," Heather Shupp of University Communications said. "Ball State has not gotten any information referring to him as a threat."

Moore, however, told NewsLink that she informed the Office of the President at BSU about the encounter with Donovan and that they had her talk to a university lawyer. The school suggested she look into obtaining a restraining order against Donovan. Officials told her BSU would take action only with a formal complaint from Moore herself.

However, Moore was not able to get a restraining order against Donovan because of changes in state law that have restricted the use of the orders to very specific groups of people, like former husbands and wives.

"They said that this [the trial process] could take up to a year, and who's to say that this won't happen again within the next year to someone else," Moore asked.

Donovan did not wish to comment for this story and his lawyer could not be reached for comment despite numerous attempts over two days by NewsLink Indiana to reach him.

Prosecutor Eric Hoffman expects a hearing to come in the next week to determine a trial date.

Figure 2.3 *Cont'd.*

References

Dailey, L., Demo, L., & Spillman, M. (2003). *The convergence continuum: A model for studying collaboration between media newsrooms.* Paper presented at the Association for Education in Journalism and Mass Communication Conference, Kansas City, MO.

35

1 At a 9 a.m. editorial story meeting, the producers and assignment editor must determine how to cover a planned news event. One of the area's U.S. senators plans a 1 p.m. news conference to announce whom he is backing for governor in the upcoming primary election. How would you cover this for the Web, TV, radio, and print? What is the best way for various producers to use their media to tell the story?

2 At 2 p.m., a car crashes into a house. How do you cover this as a breaking story for all media? And how do you cover it when it's no longer breaking? In a short paper, outline what you plan to cover, what resources you plan to use, and why you would take this approach. Spend some time with that last part, making sure to justify your expenditure of resources.

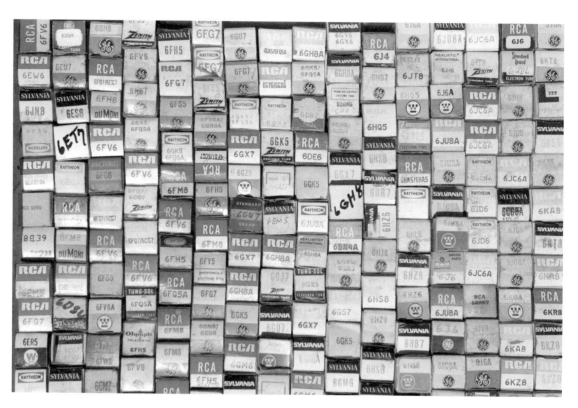

A tub of various tubes for old radios or television sets sits at a vendor's lot at the Hamfest at the Monroe County Fairgrounds outside Monroe, Michigan, Sunday, June 20, 2004. (Photograph courtesy of Amanda Goehlert.)

Words: The Foundation Stone of Journalism

What difference does it make if you live in a picturesque little outhouse surrounded by 300 feeble minded goats and your faithful dog . . .? The question is: Can you write?

—Ernest Hemingway

A good friend and office mate of mine had this quote taped to the door of our office for several years. It stuck with me long after we parted company, not because of the question itself, but because of the writing that sets up the question. "A picturesque little outhouse" is a phrase we wouldn't normally turn these days. "Feeble minded goats?" Same deal. In asking "Can you write?" Hemingway shows us the benefits of writing itself.

With the proliferation of Internet sites that promote open expression, a great many voices that would not otherwise have been heard can now reach large audiences. For example, the Drudge Report has gained acceptance in some media circles while still operating outside of mainstream journalism. Others, with varying degrees of success, have also issued reporting-style Web sites.

Student Web pages can serve as posting boards for everything from Spring Break pictures to political manifestos. A number of Web sites have turned content provision over to readers, allotting space for individuals to host Web logs, or *blogs* as they are more commonly known. This proliferation of media options appears to have created a true mass media in which everyone has a voice. The millions of words added to the Internet each day demonstrates that people can fill space with thoughts and ideas. It also demonstrates that a lot of people can type. But can they write? The answer to that question is still up for debate.

A quick scan of any one of these sites would bring a fourth-grade English teacher to tears. Misspellings, grammar problems, and a general lack of clarity are common. Perhaps the speed at which the ideas can become postings contributes to the lack of coherent thought and well-crafted writing. Perhaps the lack of editorial oversight leads to the stream of errors and incomplete thoughts. Perhaps we need to go back to the basics and assess how fervently and accurately we can answer Hemingway's question.

The purpose of this chapter is to outline why writing is important in the age of the Internet, discuss some simple approaches to shaping your writing, and provide you with a process for editing your work before it goes out for public consumption. This isn't meant to be the definitive guide for writing, but it should at least outline why the skills of a newspaper journalist are valuable to journalists in all media.

Technology and Toys Can't Save You

A group of researchers from the University of South Florida set out on a mission in 2002: to find out what people who hire journalists want to see in a potential employee and to assess how important convergence had become in journalism. The study surveyed hundreds of people involved in journalism to ask what types of skills were most critical in determining the success of a journalist.

The authors found that, even with technological options such as multimedia production, the respondents overwhelmingly chose good writing as the number one skill students needed if they hoped to get a job in the field. A quote from one editor demonstrated how extreme the need for good writing was: "I've worked in markets 170 to 20 and having training in multiple media will not help you get a job, but being a good writer will" (Huang *et al.*, 2003).

Another study interviewed instructors from eight colleges with national reputations for their journalism programs. The researchers asked instructors about the value of convergence and whether it belonged in the curriculum. Two factions formed: those who put a great deal of faith in convergence and those who thought it less critical on the media landscape. One thing both groups could agree on, however, was that an emphasis on journalistic writing mechanics, journalistic style, and English grammar were key to all good journalism programs (Bulla & Dodd, 2003). Additional work in this area (Bulla, 2002; Zoch & Collins, 2003) has approached this topic with a variety of ideas and a variety of spins. In the end, however, the importance of good writing has prevailed.

How to Write Well

Reporting comes first: To make your writing sing, you'll need to do some strong reporting before you do anything else. Far too often, students (and many journalists) think, "I'll write around that." Unfortunately, if you approach reporting that way, you severely limit your ability to write. Reporting is at the core of all good stories. You must learn as much about the topic as possible so that you are well versed in what you are going to write about. You must do as much of this research as possible in advance so that you know what questions to ask and how to pursue the issue. You must be willing to ask questions of a source more than once and feel free to follow up with fresh questions as they arise in your writing. Here's a simple set of guidelines for how to best set up your writing:

41

- *Background:* Do as much research as you can about the person, place, or thing you are going to be writing about. Look for stories other people have done on this topic. Ask your colleagues what they know about this topic. If an editor assigned you this story, ask why the editor thought this was important and if he or she has any ideas on where you should look for background. Do library research on a topic so that you can have an intelligent conversation with your source about it. Some journalists have immersed themselves in the activities they are about to cover, which allows them to convey with more precision and clarity exactly what the subject is going through. You don't need to go that far, but you can if you feel it will help you. It's all up to you. It is OK not to know as much about the topic as the person you are interviewing. It is inexcusable to know almost nothing. Don't think you can fake it. If you do, chances are the source will sniff that out and be less helpful. No matter how you go about preparing for your next assignment, the more you know before you start, the better off you will be.

- *Interviews:* Make sure you talk not only to a good number of people, but also people with a wide array of perspectives. Some educators and journalists say that you should get as many "sides" as possible, but in setting yourself up that way, you might lose out on some good perspectives. Only interviewing people for or against something sets them in opposition to each other. It also tends to paint an issue in black or white and ignore the subtle grays. This kind of broad view is especially important for personality profiles. Think of the professor who is teaching your class, for example. As a student, you view that professor in a certain way. Perhaps the person is an authority figure. Perhaps the person is viewed as a good leader. Perhaps the person is viewed as ruling with an iron fist. No matter how many students you interview, the perspective will always be limited by that student–teacher relationship. By expanding the list of interview subjects, you can find out more about this teacher. What does your teacher's boss think of him or her? Would your teacher's spouse add a different perspective? Friends, relatives, and coworkers all provide some interesting views on your subject. Even the most powerful person in the world has a mother.

- *Never enough:* In many cases, time is a huge factor in what you can gather. Daily deadlines, late-breaking news, and other delights prevent you from getting as much information as you would like. As one of my favorite journalism teachers used to say, "Journalism is never done. It's just due." However, when you have the opportunity to get more information, take advantage. You might not use it all, but you're better off having it and not needing it than needing it and not having it. Get the extra source or the extra document and you'll feel secure in what you are working on. You also want to make sure that you get additional contact information from your sources, if possible. This will allow you to contact them outside of the office if you run into more questions as your story develops.

- *Deeper is better:* Depth doesn't always mean unearthing a scandal and bringing it to light. Depth means a richness of reporting that can allow the reader to experience the story in a variety of ways. For example, don't tell the readers that a fire damaged a house. Show your readers the charred frame, the blackened windows, and the grimy soot that permeates every inch of the rickety remains. Give the readers a big sniff of the horrible stench emanating from the structure. Allow your readers feel the crunch of the burnt wood the firefighters walked over as they fought the blaze. Report with all of your senses and you'll help your audience feel more deeply connected to the scene.

Welcome Back, Old Friend

For what seems like an interminable number of years, writers, editors, and educators have been sounding the death knell of the inverted pyramid. It's been called boring, among other things, and yet for some reason, trend after trend in journalism has been unable to unseat it. The immediacy-based approach to journalism that the Web requires seems to have resuscitated the inverted pyramid.

The inverted pyramid is a simple form of writing that attempts to address the legendary "five Ws and one H" of journalism. (For those of you who don't know or can't recall, they are *who, what, when, where, why,* and *how*.) It is used to pack the top of the story with as much information as possible and tells the story, with the most important paragraph at the top and the least important one at the bottom.

Notice that the last sentence says "least important," not "unimportant." Regardless of how much space in which you have to operate, there should never be an unimportant paragraph. Each paragraph should, in some way, add value to the story. In newspapers, space is finite, with a limited number of inches available for all the stories that need to go into the paper. On the Web, space is infinite, but just because the space is available, it doesn't mean you should use it. An overly long story can be just as boring on a Web site as it is in a newspaper or magazine. Furthermore, the medium itself screams for immediacy.

In using the inverted pyramid, you learn how to prioritize information and give the readers what they want to know most, first. People who get their news from the Web are often racing through the Internet and will need something truly great to stop them in their tracks. You want to make sure that you've got the most interesting and important information high enough that it does just that. No one is going to stop for a story that starts off with "Smithville Zoo keepers reported Monday an incident involving an animal." However, this opening is likely to get a second look: "The largest python in captivity disappeared from the

Smithville Zoo on Monday, only to be found three hours later sleeping on a school bus."

It's not about being sensational, but rather about letting people know what happened that will change their lives. No one cared that the city council met Monday to discuss a number of city issues. They want to know if their taxes are going up, if the roads are getting fixed, or if a controversial construction project is going to happen. If you think about what matters most, you will provide readers with the news they want.

Even if you don't end up writing in a purely inverted pyramid fashion, it helps to think that way. By prioritizing the information in your mind, you can figure out what matters most. You might decide to use a narrative topper or an example near the beginning of your story. You might not have a clear-cut top news item to lead with. You might have so much information that it becomes difficult to choose one piece of information with which to start the story. If you order your thoughts in inverted pyramid fashion, chances are you will serve the public better.

44

Putting It Together

All forms of writing require a basic structure that allows the reader to see a beginning, a middle, and an end. Fairy tales open with "Once upon a time" and close with "The end." Letters and e-mails open with "Dear so-and-so" and close with a signature (be it electronic or hand-written). Jokes open with "Did you hear the one about . . ." and close with laughter (you hope). Journalism has its established norms as well when it comes to the openings of stories, the middle information, and the closing paragraph.

The Lead: Sounding the Opening Bell

The beginning is traditionally the lead of the story. Whether it's a strict inverted pyramid lead or a feature-style approach, the opening of the story is meant to engage the reader and move him or her into the rest of the story. Lead sentences for news stories tend to try to capture the who, what, when, where, why, and how of a story. Since the sentence should be between 25 and 35 words, not all of those elements always end up in the lead. The elements that end up in the lead should be there for a reason. Those that don't should be omitted for a reason. Beginning journalists often have problems deciding what should be included and what shouldn't. When it comes to writing, no hard-and-fast rules exist.

It is best to answer the questions you think will arise in a reader's mind. Good writers always have good reasons for the choices they make.

Look for the elements you think matter the most. Seek out the best way to present accurate information and simultaneously grab your reader's attention. Don't waste time with things people couldn't care less about. For example, imagine coming home and your roommate tells you, "Your mom called. Your dad was in a car accident." If you screamed, "What happened?" and your roommate started with "The Centerville Police Department responded to a report of an accident..." you'd likely cut your roommate off in midsentence and demand to know if anyone was hurt, how bad the damage was, and what caused the crash. When seen in those terms, what should come first seems to be common sense. Yet, when rookie journalists sit down to write their first accident brief, their lead usually starts with "The Centerville Police Department responded...."

Gaining a Sense of Closure
The end should let people know that the story has officially closed. There should be no doubt that the reader has reached the end of the line. Far too often, stories end because the writer has just decided to stop writing. In other forms of writing, this would not be acceptable. Imagine how irate readers of a murder mystery novel would be if the writer just decided to quit writing before unveiling the killer. Completing a task is not the same as just being done. The end should seek either to wrap up what has happened or look forward to the next event in the story line.

In terms of wrapping up, a closing quote can be particularly helpful and valuable. In many cases, a source talking about a topic can sum it up better than you can as a writer. One of the big drawbacks of trying to do a summary on your own is that it comes across as forced or phony. With a quote, the person not only sums up what you need, but often does it in a more sincere manner.

If you decide not to close your story with a quote, look for things that give your readers a look ahead to the next part of the story. A simple wrap-up and look forward can be as simple as "The city council will vote on the issue during its July 9 meeting" or "All proceeds from the event will benefit the Smithville Charity Network." By bringing closure to the story, you let your readers know that you've completed the story and they can move on.

45

Making a Middle Matter

Most beginning journalists understand the idea of a beginning and an end. Most of them, however, don't understand what makes a middle work. The middle of a story needs to be more than the opportunity to kill off some space until you can get from that great lead to that killer closing quote. You must make your middle matter.

Journalists tend to make it more difficult than it needs to be when they put the middle together. A common phenomenon among journalists is that of "notebook emptying," which leads to overly long stories with flabby middles. Too often, writers find themselves attached to the material they have gathered, leading them to put every last detail in the story.

Details are good when they help tell the story. However, using details for the sake of using details creates problems. In newspapers or magazines, space constraints tend to curtail the journalistic desire to empty every last scrap of information from a reporter's notebook. The expansive nature of the Web is both a benefit and a curse. While it opens the doors to longer and longer stories, it doesn't guarantee that those stories will be any better than their truncated colleagues.

To make sure your middle matters, go back to the rules that govern the inverted pyramid: Facts should be organized in descending order of importance. Make sure that each fact adds to and supports the lead. Sometimes, a few worthless sentences creep into the middle and hide there. Weed them out and give your readers only the key stuff.

Make sure that there is enough background information to make the reader understand the story, even if they haven't seen a story on this topic before. An editor once gave me a simple test that allowed me to see if I had provided my readers with enough information: Imagine your reader is a businessperson on a trip from California to New York. The traveler has to change planes in your city and happens to grab a copy of the local paper on the way to a connecting flight. In the middle of the rest of the flight to New York, the person reads your story. Is there enough background in that story to allow that reader to follow your story? If not, go back and add more.

Finally, read each sentence and then state, "This matters because..." and fill in the rest. You should be able to say things like "This matters because it shows how much damage the fire did to the house" or "This matters because it tells people when the next presidential debate will be on television." Make sure that you really try to take your story apart, piece by piece. In the end, you'll find that the middle is trim and strong, giving your readers only what they need to know.

The Editing Process

Writing and editing are complementary processes. In an ideal world, editing begins with the writer. Throughout the process, the writer should have a hand in guiding the story until everyone involved is happy with the finished product. In most cases, however, deadline pressure, communication breakdowns, and daily newsroom life tend to get in the way. Even with the problems that can impede the work of both writer and editor, it is important to understand that writers and editors are not sworn enemies. Some writers view editing as a process that requires them to defend their work against unwarranted intrusion by an editor. Meanwhile, some editors see stories as pieces of critically wounded journalism that a writer dumped on the editing desk, assuming the editor would be able to pump life back into it. While these are extreme cases, writers and editors tend to view each other through a wary eye.

47

Writer as Editor

The first and best editors are always the writers themselves. As a writer, you are expected to be the expert on the topic you're examining. While editors are there to help you shape your vision, no one in the newsroom should know as much about this story as you. For that reason, you need to have a conversation with yourself after you've finished that first draft.

You need to stop looking at the story as a writer and start looking at it as an editor. Do your best to poke holes in the story. Look for places where you might have missed a fact or two. Shore up the weak spots with additional research, another quote, or through an extra phone call to a source. Print the story and read it on paper. You'll see a ton of minor problems you didn't notice when you were looking at it on the screen. Read the story out loud. When you verbalize what you've written, you'll notice if you've used the same word five times in one sentence. You'll also notice if the sentence is constructed properly or if you missed a word or two. Reading your work aloud is another way to spot check yourself for things that might have slipped past you during the writing stage.

Use a dictionary. Journalists sometimes use bigger words to make themselves sound more important or to make their writing sound more serious. In many cases, the words do not mean what the journalist thinks they mean. Rather than look the word up, they let it go. When you start the self-editing process, take the time to look the word up. The dictionary isn't made of a toxic material, so it won't hurt you when you pull it off the shelf, blow the dust off of it, and try to find out exactly what "pejorative" means. Your readers and your editor will ultimately thank you.

The importance of writer as editor cannot be understated, especially in the world of the Internet. In many cases, putting information online means a rush to get it up there fast. You need to make sure you are giving yourself a strong edit because it might be the only heavy edit the piece gets. If you are writing for a personal Web site or a blog, you might not have anyone to act as your editor. If it's all you, make sure you are your harshest critic because it's your reputation.

Editing versus Fixing

Many reporters (and more than a few editors) have the misperception that editors should be fixing copy. First drafts covered in comments, questions, and general scrawl marks are common sights in newsrooms. However, editing and fixing are not the same thing and far too often we find editors doing fixes rather than making edits. This robs the writer of a valuable learning opportunity and it does little to alter future behavior. Simply put, fixing is where the editor pulls up a story on the computer and attacks it with speed and fury. Punctuation is changed, sentences are rewritten, and paragraph order is shifted. Even if the editor hands an amended story back to the reporter for a rewrite, the process remains one of fixing rather than editing.

The keys to editing are collaboration and a common goal. The collaborative process works best when the editor and the reporter examine the story from a detached place, discuss the merits of the work, and provide a solid analysis as to what needs to be fixed and why.

Perhaps the most important part of the preceding sentence is the last word: "why." Without a general understanding as to why something needs to be changed, writers never grow and editors never see true improvement. Instead, writers end up digging in their heels and fighting against change. Editors never get the best story possible from the reporter. The "why" component is vital. Think about any conversation you've ever had with a parent or a teacher that went poorly. You might have been told you couldn't do something you wanted to do.

When you asked why, the answer might have come back, "Because I said so. That's why." If you think back on that moment, it probably seemed a fairly unsatisfactory answer because you weren't able to understand the rationale behind what you were told. When it comes to writing, an editor who tells you to fix something "because I said so" deprives you of any ability to incorporate those changes into your view of writing. Granted, sometimes deadlines and other forms of impending doom require a brusque response. However, after the danger has passed, it would probably be beneficial to inquire as to why you were asked to make a change.

Similarly, you should have a good answer when an editor asks the "why" question. Being able to rationalize behavior is a two-way street when it comes to editing. An editor is seeing a story for the first time and, thus, acts like a reader would. The editor sees the story unfold and wonders why certain facts are missing or why certain pieces are higher in the story than others. Readers will have those questions as well. If there is a logical reason behind what you've done, you can discuss the issue with your editor from a much stronger position. Sometimes, we do things "just because," which doesn't exactly inspire confidence in our editors. In that final read before you take the story to the editor, go over your story and ask yourself why you included certain things and why you chose that particular order for those things. It will help you work better with your editor in getting the point across.

The "Final" Edit

Once you and your editor decide that the pieces are all in place, you're still not done. You need to give your story one final read for all the minor things (and a few major ones) that can cause you trouble once the story has been disseminated to the masses. Go through the story on paper again and perhaps even read it out loud again. If you've moved pieces around, you might have pulled a quote above the material that introduces the source. With computers, it's easy to move text around, but it's also easy to move things you didn't intend to move.

When you're reading the piece, have your source material handy. Check names, addresses, titles, and spellings. Make sure the numbers are all right. Also keep your AP style guide and dictionary handy. You might catch that numerical error or realize you used the wrong word. Each time you read something, you'll notice another minor thing or two. Clean them up as best you can, given the time available.

Once you've completed this final read, take a deep breath and let the story go. You can drive yourself crazy second-guessing what you've done. Instead, realize you did the best with what you had and move on. For most journalists, feedback on a story gives them something to use for their next story. Web journalists, however, can rework and redo their copy as they learn more about a story or as a story develops. Changes can be made throughout the life of a Web story. During each "final" edit, you should go through the steps discussed in this chapter to ensure that you've got the best and most accurate product available for your readers. Regardless of the format, accuracy remains the number one goal of all journalistic writing.

Conclusion

This chapter outlines how to approach writing for print media and any Web extensions of print. It is meant to lay the foundation for what you'll be seeing later in this book and also later in your journalism courses.

Writing is a craft and must be honed over time. It's like any other activity you've taken part in. Could you make 100 free throws in a row the first time you picked up a basketball? Probably not. Many professionals can't do that. Still, the people who spend a lot of time practicing are likely to make more shots than those people who don't put in the practice time. The point is, just because you've been "writing" all your life doesn't mean this type of writing will come easily to you.

Writing for a news outlet is different than writing a research paper, an e-mail, a letter, or a work of fiction. It takes a special attention to detail and the ability to focus on what matters most to readers. The more time you spend writing and reporting, the more likely these things will come naturally to you. In the meantime, don't be discouraged as you work toward consistency. Eventually, you will feel more confident answering the question "Can you write?" with a resounding "Yes!"

References

Bulla, D. (2002). *Media convergence: Industry practices and implications for education.* Paper presented at the Association for Education in Journalism and Mass Communication Conference, Miami, FL.

Bulla, D., & Dodd, J. (2003). *Convergence writing instruction: Interviews with journalism faculty members about curriculum decisions.* Paper presented at the Association for Education in Journalism and Mass Communication Conference, Kansas City, MO.

Huang, E., Davison, K., Shreve, S., Davis, T., Bettendorf, E., & Nair, A. (2003). *Facing the challenges of convergence*. Paper presented at the Association for Education in Journalism and Mass Communication Conference, Kansas City, MO.

Zoch, L., & Collins, E. (2003). *Preparing for a career in the unknown: What convergent newsroom managers want and need*. Paper presented at the Association for Education in Journalism and Mass Communication Conference, Kansas City, MO.

51

1 Find a newspaper story in your local or school paper and dissect it. In a short paper, identify the "five Ws and one H" in your chosen story and then explain the importance of each. For example, was the "who" more important than the "how"? Explain if the beginning, middle, and end each did its job. Was the middle flabby? Was there enough background information to help you understand the story? Did the story close well or did it just end? Make a case as to whether this story was well written. Include a copy of the article you dissected with your paper.

2 Find a public place such as a park or a shopping mall and spend at least 20 minutes observing your surroundings. Then write a short story about what you saw. Make sure it has a beginning, a middle, and an end. When you are explaining what happened, look for ways to show your audience what you observed. Don't worry about interviews or getting sources for this exercise. Focus on your senses. What did it sound like? What smells were present? Was it warm and sunny or snowy and cold? The story likely won't be very newsworthy, but that's OK. The purpose of this exercise is to help you work on structure and description.

A first-grade boy presses play on the cassette that matches the book he has chosen to read during a literacy session in class at an elementary school in Columbia, Missouri. The sessions focus on integrating phonics, sight, sound, and reading to gain a deeper understanding of words. (Photograph courtesy of Amanda Goehlert.)

Broadcast Writing and Speaking

Writing for broadcast is unlike almost any kind of writing you might have done before. That's because of the fundamental differences inherent in both the transmission and reception of broadcasting—both radio and television. Information that is broadcast involves people saying the information out loud while the audience takes it all in by virtue of hearing it. Broadcast is spoken on the one hand and heard on the other. It's as simple—and as complicated—as that.

Almost everything we do in constructing messages for broadcast ultimately comes down to producing words that can be spoken well and understood by people who only get to hear them. Those two aspects of broadcast lead to a world of challenges.

In print, readers can reread material. They can stop and mull over what they read or check another source. None of those options is available in broadcast. The reporter or anchor says the material one time—at a pace determined by the reporter or anchor. The audience gets one shot and one shot only at understanding what's being said. The audience can't go back for another pass. Viewers and listeners have no chance to think over and decipher something that might be unclear.

Those differences in delivery and understandability result in forming broadcast messages (news) differently than print. It's neither better nor worse. It's just different. As a broadcast journalist, you must first think about how to say the material out loud. In print, we have a series of stylistic rules so that every time the reader encounters a name or reference, its usage is consistent and therefore not confusing. In broadcast, where most of the audience never sees the copy, we have rules for writing designed to make reading the copy easier for the anchor and reporter. This chapter explores the ways in which broadcast writing is tailored for the ear.

Rules for Readability

The following subsections cover guidelines for making copy more clear for broadcast announcers.

Page Form

Copy to be read on the air is double spaced—sometimes triple spaced. In radio, copy is written all across the page (with standard margins). In television, use a split page with audio (the script) on the right and video (supers and instructions) on the left.

Numbers

Single digits on a page are too easily lost, and some looks like letters. Write out numbers *one* through *nine*; use numerals for *10* through *999*; then use the appropriate combination of numerals and words for thousand, million, and so on. Ordinals can go either way (*second* or *2nd*). Years should be written as numerals.

Abbreviations

Don't use abbreviations in broadcast writing. Abbreviations require translation in order to read, and that poses the potential for stumbling. In addition, some abbreviations stand for more than one thing (*St.*, for example). Exceptions include *Mr.*, *Mrs.*, and *Dr.* We see them so often and they always precede names, so there's little danger of mispronunciation.

Symbols

Don't use symbols. They require translation and, in the case of the dollar sign ($), appear in a different place than when they're read out loud.

Acronyms and Initials

An acronym involves letters to be read as a word, such as *OPEC*. In that case, use all caps with no dashes. Initials are to be read as a series of individual letters, such as *I-R-S*. In that case, use all caps with dashes in between the letters. Note that in the case of most acronyms and initials, you should use the full name of the organization on the first reference and the initials or the acronym for subsequent references.

Sentence Length

Keep sentences short. Go back to those two keys points that separate broadcast from print: Read out loud and understand by being heard. Keep the sentence length short because an announcer can only read so many words at one time without pausing to breathe. We write short sentences to build breathing into the process. An unnatural pause (breathing) in a sentence could make the copy difficult to understand.

Sound

Radio and television journalists are in the sound business, so we must think about sound. That's a dimension that isn't available in print. Because we say things out loud, the sound those syllables and words make helps convey meaning. For that matter, we can convey meaning simply by how we say something. If you're not using those aspects of writing, then you're not fully utilizing the strengths of the medium. Where possible, choose words that sound like what they mean: *buzz*, *snap*, *tap*, and so on. Try to choose hard-sounding words to express hard messages. *Kill*, with its hard *k* sound, emphasizes the message of the meaning.

At the same time, there are sounds that are awkward or harder to pronounce. The soft *h* sound of words that begin with *h* may be a bit awkward for some people to pronounce. You have to pause to reshape your mouth to pronounce the soft *h* sound properly. That doesn't mean you have to avoid those words. It does mean that a word beginning with a soft *h* must clearly be the best choice for the sentence. Watch out for difficult sound combinations, like *sks*. The word *desks*, for example, is difficult to pronounce. You can create the problem with the *sks* combination simply by unfortunate placement: *Task says* creates the same problem even though the *sks* group is in separate words. The point is that how something sounds matters, both for pronunciation as well as meaning. Pay attention to sound, and remember that you're never done with a piece of copy until you've tested it by reading it aloud.

Pronouncers

Any word that might be mispronounced requires a pronouncer—a pronunciation guide. Written after the name within parentheses, it's a phonetic guide for someone who doesn't know how to pronounce the name. Calais, Maine, would be written as *Calais (CAL us), Maine.* Don't substitute phonetic spelling for real spelling. That will trip up people who know how to pronounce the name, and it's why we periodically see the phonetic spelling written across the bottom of the screen instead of the correct spelling. This only applies to proper names. If you're planning to use a word that isn't a proper name but that you think might be mispronounced, you need to evaluate why you're using that word.

All of the preceding rules are designed with the notion that announcers should be able to pick up any piece of broadcast copy—even one they have never seen before—and read it well. In an ideal world, that would never actually happen. In the real world of broadcast, it happens all the time. Anchors have a much better chance of reading copy well if it conforms to those rules of readability.

Rules for Understandability

We need to construct messages in such a way that someone who only gets to hear the material—and gets to hear it once—can understand it. We need to do this within a framework that recognizes that as passive media, radio listeners or television viewers might be splitting their attention among multiple tasks. Guidelines for enhancing understandability follow.

Informal

We don't write broadcast copy exactly the way we speak, but it's close. Spoken language is a bit too casual and frequently not grammatically correct. Broadcast copy is what we wish we had said if we collected and organized our thoughts properly and cleaned it up to make it right *before* we said anything. The writing, however, remains informal, and it's just fine to use more casual terms like *kids* instead of *children*.

Word Choice

Good writing is all about good word choice and proper ordering of those words. Since this is journalism, the first rule for word choice is accuracy. The word has to be right. Not close to right. Not nearly right. Absolutely right. Next, the word has to be appropriate for the context. Remember the audience only gets to hear the information and only gets to hear it once. Every word that you use has to be clear and understandable instantly in the context in which you're using the word. Whatever meaning a word conjures in the minds of the listeners is the way you should use it. That means defending word choice based on its fourth dictionary definition probably isn't going to cut it. Use words the way they're commonly used.

Numbers

There are certain rules for how to write numbers so that an announcer can read them. On the other side of the coin, it's critical to understand that people generally don't take in and process numbers well when they only get to hear them. Keep numbers at a minimum in broadcast copy so you don't leave the audience behind. Obviously, if the story is about a tax increase, you're going to have to use numbers. But think about whether the audience needs to know that *96 out of 100 students passed the test*, or whether you could just say *almost all*. Along those lines, rounding numbers can help an audience better understand the material. For example, it's easier to process the phrase *more than a thousand* than it is to grapple with *1,012*. Even in television, where it's possible to put numbers on the screen where people can read them, minimize the use of numbers.

Contractions

We speak in contractions, and generally it's acceptable to use them in broadcast copy, with two exceptions. First, do not use them if the meaning might be missed. The difference between *can* and *can't* is an announcer's ability to pronounce the *t* sound clearly and the audience to hear that—although the meanings are opposite. Other contractions with *not* don't present as much of a problem. So always spell out *can not*.

Second, you might want to emphasize the *not* part of the expression, in which case you wouldn't contract it: *He said he did NOT commit the crime.*

Titles before Names

In broadcast, we put titles and identifiers before the name. That's because what people need to know is the title—which is likely why we're talking with someone. The name itself is detail that is less critical to understanding the story. We also tend to shorten titles. No need to do that for nice, short, self-explanatory titles, but we commonly change a long obscure title into a short description of what the audience needs to know (e.g., *a state welfare official* rather than some long, involved title). We also tend to shorten names in two ways: First, don't use middle names or initials unless the person is commonly known that way—and few people are. Second, we tend to use a shortened first name if people are commonly known or go by the shortened name, rather than their formal name. Consequently, *Joseph* frequently becomes *Joe*—assuming the person goes by *Joe*.

Attribution before the Statement

Broadcast generally puts attribution—the source of information—before the statement or information. That's because the source determines how we look at or think about any piece of information. In broadcast, we can't afford to have the audience mulling over the source and reevaluating the information because we continue reading. Therefore, it is more important to say right up front that Superintendent of Schools Joe Smith is the source who thinks the school board should vote on a plan to close a school. The title and source give the statement more credibility than if it were made by angry parent John Doe. Telling people the source of information before presenting the facts makes it clearer and easier to digest the information when people only get to hear it.

One Idea or Thought per Sentence

We also keep sentences short for the sake of the audience. People can only take in so much information at one time when they only get to hear it. Each sentence in broadcast should contain no more than one important thought or idea. If you have more than one key point,

60

you have an overloaded sentence that will be harder to read and much harder to understand. Split up the information into separate sentences.

Voice and Tense

Use active voice wherever possible. In active voice, the subject of the sentence does the action as opposed to passive voice, where the subject of the sentence receives the action. Active is shorter, tighter, punchier, and more interesting. Our first choice in tense is present. Broadcast is all about what's going on now, so present tense plays to that strength. Second choice is future tense. Third choice is present perfect, which uses "has" and "have" to indicate that some activity, while in the past, took place recently.

Leads

The lead, the opening sentence of a story, is by far the most important sentence in the story. But the broadcast lead isn't at all like the print lead and doesn't serve the same purpose. In fact, the broadcast lead most closely parallels the print headline. The sole job of the broadcast lead is to get the attention of the audience just as the print headline's job is to direct the reader to the story. The lead may also convey information about the story, but that's not its critical function. It's all about getting the attention of the listener or viewer. Consequently, the lead must be short, strong, and interesting.

Chronological Story Development

Not all stories have a chronology, that is, one event taking place after another. When a story has that chronological development, the story is almost always best told that way. That fits right into the traditional oral storytelling tradition. We start with the lead—Say, *did you hear about X?*—then we tell the story from beginning to end. It's easiest to remember the details that way, and it's easier for the listener to understand the story development that way.

If there is no chronological development, however, the story's sequence still needs to make sense. It's not a random collection of facts. You will never collect all of your information in the exact same sequence in which you will tell the story, so you need to look at the pieces you've gathered and determine the proper order of facts. Start with a strong lead to get people's attention, and then figure out how you're going to tell the story, going logically and as linearly as possible, through the facts of the story. That works for hard news. Features are different and harder to tell because you have to build in surprises and interesting aspects of the story periodically throughout the material.

The preceding rules are designed to give the listener or viewer a fighting chance at understanding what the broadcaster is saying.

Story Formats

Radio stories' typologies are categorized by the origin of the sound used within them. There's the *reader*, which is simply the newscast announcer reading a story. In commercial radio, a reader isn't likely to run more than 15 to 20 seconds. In public radio, it might go double that. We dress up stories through the use of *natural sound* (also called *nat sound, wild sound,* or *ambient sound*) and *actualities*. Natural sound is the sound of real life, recorded onto tape or disk. It might be the sound of chanting protesters, honking car horns, or the growl of a tiger. Actualities are the comments of people in the news. We might capture those by recording a teacher talking to her class or by interviewing the mayor. A *voicer* is a story recorded by a reporter, as opposed to one that is read by the announcer. In commercial radio, a voicer isn't likely to run more than 20 to 30 seconds. In public radio, a voicer might go 40 to 50 seconds. A *wrap* or *wraparound* is a voicer with one or more actualities or pieces of natural sound included, which allows for greater depth and length. In commercial radio, a wrap might go 45 seconds to a minute. Public radio wraps can run up to 2 to 3 minutes or even longer. A *live* report, occasionally called a *ROSR* or *radio on scene report,* is the final category of radio news.

Television stories are divided by complexity. The simplest form is the *TV reader*. A TV reader is essentially a radio story read by the anchor on television. The one potential complication of the reader is television's use of box graphics—that over-the-shoulder box that includes a visual related to the story. Even with box graphics, the story is still a reader, but the graphics may change how the story is written. Without the graphics, there would be no difference in the wording between a radio reader and a TV reader. With the graphics, the first line of the story must also reference whatever is in the box. If the box says "robbery," then the lead must include that information. If the box includes a picture of the mayor, then the lead must include the mayor's name. As with radio, TV readers usually don't run longer than 15 to 20 seconds.

The next level of TV complexity is the *voiceover* or VO. With VOs, the anchor usually starts reading on camera and then continues to read as the audience sees video that relates to the content of the story. Most voiceovers don't run beyond 30 to 40 seconds, but the story and interest of the pictures will ultimately determine length.

The next level of complexity is the *VO/SOT* and includes variants such as VO/SOT/VO or SOT/VO or just SOT. This type of TV story is a mixture of voiceover with sound on tape. As with a VO, it typically starts with the anchor on camera, then the anchor continues to talk while the audience sees video, then the story goes to someone talking on tape. That's usually a bite or sound bite—the TV equivalent of the radio actuality.

The *package* or pack is a prerecorded blend of video, bites, natural sound, reporter track, and reporter standup. Commonly, these reporter packages start with either a brief nat sound full or a short bite. They then go to the reporter talking over the video that we're seeing. Bites and additional material spoken by the reporter are also woven into the package. Somewhere within that package, we usually have a reporter standup, where we see and hear the reporter talking. These days, reporter packages tend to run a minute and a quarter to a minute and a half, but some stations still run packages that are up to two and a half minutes long.

The last TV category is the *live* report. Sometimes, this simply involves a reporter on location talking about something that is happening or just happened. More commonly, it involves a reporter live on location introducing and then wrapping up a prerecorded package. Typically, these reports start with the anchor introducing the story. We then see what's called a *double box* with the anchor in one box on the screen and a reporter in the other box. As the reporter starts to speak, we switch to the reporter full screen who continues live. On a set roll cue, the station runs the video of the reporter package that has been put together earlier. When the package is over, instead of the standard, prerecorded package outcue (something like, "Alyssa Jones, Channel 8 News, downtown"), we go back to the reporter live on location who wraps up the story. In many cases, we go back to a double box with the reporter and anchor and may go back and forth with Q&A.

63

Live reports introducing and ending packages tend to be longer than just packages, with the amount of Q&A determining total length.

A Closer Look

Take a look at this broadcast story:

> Police are searching for two men and maybe a baby who robbed a downtown convenience store last night. Maybe a baby because one of the masked men cradled what witnesses said could have been a baby in one arm—while holding a gun in the other. Police say customers and clerks were told to lie down on the floor of the Martin Quick Stop at Jackson and Main. They say the man with what might have been a baby kept his gun on the customers while the other jumped behind the counter and emptied the cash register. The two got away in what witnesses described as a 1970s-era, rusted Oldsmobile.

64

This story would work well as a radio story or television reader. Note that all the sentences are short. Note also that there is a geographic identifier in the lead. We always need that so the audience isn't left wondering where the story takes place. Note also that the unusual aspect of the story—the man with a baby—is featured right in the lead. While we work to avoid repetition of words or phrases, here we repeated a phrase, *"maybe a baby,"* because it's unusual and helps emphasize and clarify a critical point.

If we had sound from one of the witnesses, it would likely run after either the lead or line two. In radio, we would have to introduce the person speaking. In television, we would usually just run the bite and super the name and description of the speaker. In radio, the story with sound might work like this:

> Police are searching for two men and maybe a baby who robbed a downtown convenience store last night. Jane Smith was shopping for snack foods when the men came in. "I couldn't believe it. I just kept looking back and forth between the baby and the gun. At least I think it was a real baby." Police aren't sure at this point. They say customers and clerks were told to lie down on the floor of the Martin Quick Stop at Jackson and Main. They say the man with what might have been a baby kept his gun on the customers while the other man jumped behind the counter and emptied the cash register. Jane Smith said, "I have never been so scared in my life." The two got away in what witnesses described as a 1970s-era, rusted Oldsmobile.

In television, the story is more likely to look like this:

Video	Audio
Anchor close-up	Police are searching for two men and maybe a baby . . . who robbed a downtown convenience store last night.
Video of convenience store	Maybe a baby because one of the masked men cradled what witnesses said could have been a baby in one arm—while holding a gun in the other.
Sound on tape (SOT) of Jane Smith Super: Jane Smith Customer	"I couldn't believe it. I just kept looking back and forth between the baby and the gun. At least I think it was a real baby."
Video of store	Police say customers and clerks were told to lie down on the floor of the Martin Quick Stop at Jackson and Main. They say the man with what might have been a baby kept his gun on the customers while the other jumped behind the counter and emptied the cash register.
SOT of Jane Smith Video of store (outside)	"I have never been so scared in my life." The two got away in what witnesses described as a 1970s-era, rusted Oldsmobile.

That's a pretty simple, straightforward story—in this case, told as a VO/SOT/VO/SOT/VO.

The various stories and forms are the bits and pieces that then go into newscasts. The producer's job is to organize this chaos into a newscast that seems to flow and make sense.

In radio, the announcer generally puts together short newscasts that frequently include no sound at all. Since the typical radio station today has only one person in news, you're not likely to hear a lot of sound unless you have a truly tireless reporter or the station subscribes to an audio service. Radio news operations where the station actually sends a reporter out to cover an event are becoming increasingly rare and tend to be limited to all news, news/talk, some public radio stations, and a handful of others.

While radio news has generally been contracting, TV news has been steadily expanding. The typical TV station today runs about 4 hours of local news every weekday and at least an hour a day on weekends. On weekdays, stations are likely to start local news some time between 5 a.m. and 6 a.m. If they're ABC, CBS, or NBC affiliates, they are likely to run local news until the network morning news at 7 a.m. Then they do short, local cut-ins during the network news. Stations commonly run a half hour of local news at noon and then an hour and a half between 5 p.m. and 7 p.m. (the other half hour is network news) and a half hour late news at either 10 p.m. or 11 p.m., depending on the time zone.

All station newscasts include local news and weather. Sports usually runs on just the 6 p.m. news and the late news. Special segments, such as consumer, health, food, and other areas, tend to run in specific newscasts, depending on how a station structures its newscasts and the audience it's trying to reach for each program.

1 Take a story from your local or school newspaper and create a broadcast script for a 25-second reader. Focus on the elements of good broadcast writing: words that can be spoken well and understood by people who only get to hear them. Craft an attention-grabbing lead, a solid body, and a good close. Remember to follow the rules of style in terms of numbers, symbols, and other similar style items. Read it aloud and time yourself. Your story needs to run exactly 25 seconds.

2 Find 5 to 10 proper nouns from your area that you think would be difficult for someone who doesn't live in your area to pronounce. Then, write broadcast-style sentences that include the nouns and pronouncers (pronunciation guides) for each of them. Remember to follow style rules.

Children paddle back to a boat docked on the Sydney coast during the height of Christmas and New Year's vacation season, December 2003. (Photograph courtesy of Amanda Goehlert.)

Writing for the Web

The great thing about writing for the World Wide Web, or Web for short, is that it makes everyone a publisher with global reach. The kid in his bedroom on the computer after dinner is on par with the multinational company in many ways. People from California to Taiwan to Poland can read whatever a formerly unknown student has to say.

The Web is a medley of news and information produced by everyone from that kid all the way on up to award-winning professional journalists and the international companies that employ them. Because the Web is a pool that everyone can jump into, it is also a place where the rules of writing are relative to what is being said and who is saying it.

From the early days of the Web, the most common style of writing has been standard wire or newspaper style. That's because many traditional news outlets shoveled their old-media content onto the Web. That's still the case, so, in many places, the rules for writing on the Web are just the same as they are for writing in print, or only a shade different.

Slowly, however, three forces are pushing writing on the Web away from its old-media roots. The first and most powerful force is the ability to self-publish with unlimited reach. People who think they have something to report or say can do so without having to worry about anyone pushing rules of style on them. They are their own editors, and this situation leads to a looser style.

The second force promoting a change in writing style is multimedia. In the past, journalists wrote for one branch of journalism at a time. Broadcast journalists use different rules than print journalists for writing. Within broadcast and print journalism there are many subdivisions of style.

The exciting thing about the flexibility of the Web is that all types of media can come together, or converge. Print, still images, sound, moving pictures, and animation can all be used to tell the same story in a way that wasn't possible before the advent of the Web. This new reality creates a need for people who are comfortable working with many writing styles simultaneously. It also opens avenues for journalists to create new ways of writing and storytelling.

The critical eye of readers on the Web is the third force reshaping journalistic writing on the Web. It impacts everyone, from *The New York Times* to the most obscure blog, and is a result of the Web's interactive nature. The Web is interactive not in the way a video game is, but more like the ways in which people interact at a café in a close-knit neighborhood. This interactivity allows people to communicate with unprecedented speed and reach. There is a constant electronic conversation going on that has turned journalism into a two-way street, and changed the way writers approach their craft.

Traditional News Writing and the Web

An eye-tracking study done in 2000 (the Stanford Poynter Project; see http://www.poynterextra.org/et/i.htm for the full study) examined the ways in which people viewed Web pages. The majority of the subjects in their study viewed text first, not photos or graphics, which might have seemed more logical. Jakob Nielsen, who *The New York Times* once called "the guru of webpage usability," found similar use issues in his studies. These findings make it very clear that text is as important (if not more important) as any other part of a Web site.

The basis for all news writing is the inverted pyramid, with its mandate to put the most important information at the top of a printed story. News writers are required to answer the who, what, where, when, how, and why very early in the story, leaving the fine details and background for later. On the Web it is no different. In fact, it's more important to produce compact and to-the-point stories.

Text is the easiest content to produce for the Web. It's easier to distribute words via the Web than it is via the printed page. Therefore, it's not surprising that most news on the Web comes in the form of the printed word.

The first efforts by newspapers and television stations to put their content on the Web resulted in the faithful reproduction of their printed news stories and TV scripts on a Web page. This is what is derisively known as "shovelware." Shoveling something already produced for one medium into the new form of the Web is easy and cheap. Today most people in the news industry agree the Web is capable of standing on its own as a platform for news creation and delivery. The only question left to answer is "How?"

The first answer to that question is by sharpening of already familiar skills. Take everything you've learned about writing the most basic story for print and hold on tight to those rules. Nielsen has often stated that Web users aren't readers. They scan. Thus, you want to put multiple entry points into a story. The use of headlines, decks, subheads, and other "breakout" formats can give your readers the chance they need to latch on to your story and stick with it. You need to cut out flowery or promotional language and stick to the bare bones, adding detail where it makes sense.

If this sounds familiar, it might be because you've read it earlier in this book. The inverted pyramid remains one of Nielsen's preferred styles of Web writing and was a large portion of Chapter 3. To aid you here, we will review the structure of an inverted pyramid story, taking into account the special considerations you need to keep in mind when you write it for the Web.

Headline

Writing a headline is a specialized skill that most reporters are not expected to master. It's the copy editor's job in most news shops, but it is a good place to start thinking about writing for the Web. When writing a headline, less is more and the same is true of the stories themselves.

The headline is tricky because it has to do several things all at once and in a very short space. The headline must be attention grabbing and make it clear to any reader what the story is about. It also must not repeat the lead.

You must distill a story and its headline into its two most important parts. The first part of any story you need to capture is what is new.

What information didn't the reader know before but needs to know now? The second part, the part that makes an accurate headline into a great headline, requires that you capture what about the story is interesting.

Sometimes, a story is obviously interesting to everyone. A credible report alerting readers that the end of the world is 48 hours away sells itself. Most of the time, though, it's up to the reporters and editors to discern what is both new and interesting about a story on changes to the local sewer system. This is where your ability to understand a story is put to the test. You are going places in this business if you can regularly zero in on what is the most important part of a story and what makes it interesting to the broadest group of readers.

The great irony about headline writing for the Web, or any writing for the Web, is that, technically speaking, you have as much space as you want. In reality, your goal is to keep your work as short and sweet as is humanly possible.

A good headline on the Web is often, though not always, shorter than the same headline would be for the printed page.

72

Lead

Writing a lead is the second hardest part of writing any story, second only to the headline. Luckily it's a little easier on the Web because you are generally expected to be more direct. There is less room to show off your creative side.

The lead of a story should immediately reveal the most important facts, and leave the reader asking questions that will make them read on. This construction is similar to that of a good print story, but there is a difference. Web users are "impatient and fickle" to quote George Murray and Tania Costanzo's examination of site usability (see http://www.collectionscanada.ca/9/1/p1-260-e.html for the full version). If they don't find what they want right away, they're likely to go someplace else. Web readers are typically looking for specific information, while print readers are often looking to be entertained. A lead that in print may be indirect or slow to develop should be to the point and without mystery on the Web.

The lead sets the theme for any story. Everything in the story should follow logically from the theme set in the lead. The news is what is both new and interesting. If something is new but not interesting or interesting but not new, then you'll either put it lower in the story or omit it altogether.

The easiest way to make a story interesting, even a brief and to-the-point Web story, is to give it a voice. The voice a Web writer wants to give a story is the voice of the people making the news, not his or her own voice as a writer. In print, it is often considered a virtue for the reporter to develop a distinct voice. For the Web, you want to go back to basics and stick with a recounting of the most valuable facts.

Quotes are the key to giving a Web news story personality without taking the time to impose your own writing voice on the story. The second or third paragraph of a story should ideally be a quote from someone who can support the facts of the lead with the pop of emotion or the weight of experience. A good quote will make the reader interested in the story, even if the facts in the lead failed to produce much of a response.

Once the news has been delivered in the lead and the human factor has been established in the supporting quote, it's time for the "nut graph."

Nut Graph

The "nut graph" is a paragraph high up in the story, usually the fourth or fifth paragraph, that explains why the story is important. It gives the story context, and it is just another element of the way news stories have been written for years.

The headline and lead deliver the news. The first supporting quote makes you care about the story. The job of the nut graph is to tell you why you should care or why it's an important story. Again, strong similarities exist between writing for the Web and writing for print except that Web writing should be more direct and lean than writing you might find in print.

The nut graph is often used as a way to recap a long-running story like a trial. The story of the day might be that a judge has unexpectedly declared a mistrial. The lead and the quote will capture the facts and drama of the moment. The nut graph follows up the news with a brief explanation of why there was even a trial in the first place.

Once the nut graph has let the reader know that, for example, the mayor was on trial for embezzling $10 million in city funds over 6 years, you can move on to the body of the story.

Body

The body of any story is just gravy. The reader should have all of the basic facts about a story by the fourth or fifth paragraph. After that comes the details associated with the news of the day and then a more complete telling of the story from its beginning.

Quotes and facts that more fully explain the how and why of a story fill out the body as a story moves from the most relevant facts to the least relevant facts. The hardest part of writing a Web story is deciding what to keep out. Every word should have meaning. Every quote should represent something more than a statement of fact. Recognizing what is filler and what is central to the story is the key to writing a good Web story.

We've just taken a look at the structure of a basic print-style story for the Web. Each news organization differs in style and emphasis, but if you master this general framework you will be ready to adapt to the demands of most editors.

Telling Your Story through Multiple Media

The next logical step for journalism on the Web is to try to tell a cohesive story through multiple forms of media. The goal of most major news groups is to develop a reusable multimedia storytelling form, where words, sound, images, and interactivity all come together to deliver the ultimate news experience. No one has reached this goal yet.

Part of the problem is that words are the common thread linking all types of media, but styles of writing have evolved to fit each type of media. No common style of writing exists that is flexible enough to support everything from a text story to an interactive feature to a TV-style story.

Journalists are trained and employed in a single medium, whether radio or TV or print, and their work is judged by the standards of that medium. Journalism today is set up to feed talent to multiple business arms. It is not set up to prepare reporters for a world where they need to be comfortable working in all forms.

In general, print is considered to be formal and direct and is written in the past tense. It also requires the writer to convey details of appearance and circumstance that bring the story to life.

Video, on the other hand, tells a lot without loading up on words. Writing for video is all about using words that support your video. The video is the story, and the facts fill in the information not obvious from the images. This storytelling form is much more personal and informal and uses the present tense.

Both forms demand the use of active rather than passive constructions.

Captions for images, and copy for information graphics, fall somewhere in between. Their roots are in print journalism, but their writing guidelines are not so different from those for TV. Caption information is expected to fill in the gaps of what is not immediately obvious from the visual information.

These various forms of media provide a quandary for the budding journalist. Some people believe in sticking with one specialty, like reporting for TV. Others urge new journalists to dabble in a little bit of everything, from reporting for print to shooting video and recording sound.

The world of convergence is a world of creative opportunities. Those opportunities are most open to people who have more than one skill and work across styles. Journalists who are not afraid to break the mold on style, while adhering to the rules on substance and ethics, will then be the ones who will create a new form of storytelling.

The early experiments in crossing borders include TV reporters and personalities using the Web as an outlet for columns or commentary in their areas of expertise. Newspaper reporters are writing and recording voice tracks for slide shows on the Web. Radio reporters are snapping photos to go along with posts of their audio to the Web.

It is a slow process, and each branch of journalism has its own demands that must be learned and mastered.

Blogs: Do-It-Yourself Journalism

The blog represents freedom to writers, and it has recently become the new frontier of journalism and journalistic writing.

Blog, short for "web log," is just a personal online journal. At its crudest, a blog is a recounting of the banality of life. At its best, a blog is a form of personal journalism that opens the public up to a whole new role in the news business.

Defining what blogs are can be tricky. They don't follow any one set of rules, which is where the freedom comes in. They do, however, have some characteristics that most bloggers would agree on.

First, they tend to be rather personal. Blogs are very much about points of view. The objectivity prized by most American news outlets is not typical of a blog. Next, blogs tend to have short entries posted on a whim. They are often fragmentary thoughts posted in response to something experienced in real life or seen elsewhere on the Web. They are generally rendered in text, but photos, video, and audio are also increasingly common.

Their most potent characteristic is that they are two-way streets. Blogs are a way to carry on a discussion about whatever subject has its own special region of the blogosphere buzzing at the moment. The blogosphere is an ever-changing constellation of sites talking about everything under the sun. It is a place with very few boundaries where people can experiment with form, content, and language. It is the antithesis of a large news organization.

A blog is personal, direct, and interactive. It is the human voice and imagination amplified by the power of the Web. War, politics, and pop culture are all obsessed over and reported on by bloggers. You name a topic and someone probably has a blog about it.

Journalists are most interested in three types of blogs: blogs that report news, blogs that critique the news, and special-interest blogs that serve as news sources.

Blogs that report the news are the most interesting phenomenon. Many mainstream media outlets now have their own blogs, often tied to editors or news personalities.

The blogs to watch are the ones that pop up in areas where news is happening. Whether it is a revolution in one of the former Soviet republics or the war in Iraq, someone with a front-row seat is blogging about it. This is granular-level news. This is unfiltered news available to a global audience. This is the public taking over where the professional journalist can't—or won't—go. Journalists are often said to be writing the first draft of history. Bloggers caught in the middle of historic events are now writing history as it happens.

The catch is that these are amateur journalists. Their goals are varied and their motives are not always clear. Their methods are unprofessional and their stories are anecdotal. Many people in the business hesitate to even call it journalism.

While some professional journalists are skeptical of the value of bloggers as reporters, teaming hordes of bloggers are constantly hounding mainstream media about its failures, real and imagined.

Pressure from the blogosphere has already forced the media to cover stories that would otherwise have been ignored. More importantly, bloggers have even forced news groups to admit journalistic failures.

These Web-based critics range from intellectuals to political cranks. Many are screaming at the top of their lungs in a wilderness so vast that no one will ever hear them. Still, their collective voice is so powerful that it is forcing professional editors and producers to sit up and take note.

That collective power is the result of the Web's interactive nature. Bloggers don't write in a vacuum. They write about each other and link to each other's sites. They post comments directly to blogs they read, and they use all sorts of these electronic ties to coordinate their efforts to draw attention to issues they deem important. Bloggers are having an electronic discussion of the news on their own terms, without the interference of big media companies.

They are also out there talking about the rest of life, too. This is where bloggers become a useful tool for journalists trying to understand a story that they know little about. The first thread in a story dealing with a subculture—say, the world of indie music or the life of staffers on Capitol Hill—could be a blog, with its free-form language and devil-may-care attitude. Finding the right blog can take a journalist to the heart of a subject that he or she had previously only been able to observe from the outside.

77

Changing Attitudes to Fit the Web

Dedicated Web writers are a curious breed. They do most of their reporting by phone and through research on the Web. They often serve as rewrite specialists, and they rarely leave the newsroom. The reason for this is that most news organizations are working to adapt their old-media structures to the Web, rather than redesign them from scratch. Because of this, the Web writer serves as a patch between the old media and its Web site. If the work being turned out by the paper or TV reporter can't go straight to the Web, the Web writer stands ready to update the story or hammer it into a usable form.

Web writers often end up acting as writers, rewriters, editors, and content producers all on the same shift. They work off of wire copy, from notes sent in by reporters, and from research done on their own. A Web writer is the Dr. Frankenstein of the news business, building something special out of whatever pieces are available.

On the other end are the reporters in the field who are being forced to confront the Web in their approach to the job. The deadline is not the one set for the morning paper or the evening broadcast. The deadline is now. Reporters used to putting whole stories together at once for deadline are having to learn to dribble breaking stories out in small chunks, much like wire services have done for years. The Web has put all reporters on a treadmill that doesn't stop.

The learning curve for writers and reporters on the Web doesn't stop once they've learned to work together to smoothly move old-media content onto the Web in a timely manner. The next role facing journalists in the Internet age is one where talent crosses boundaries. It is one in which writers can weave together the text, sound, video, and images needed to create a modern multimedia story.

Writers in this new age need to be able to turn on a dime from laying out the facts in a straightforward text story to entertaining the public with the personality needed to carry story told through video.

Twenty years from now, the writing that will be used to produce news will have morphed into a new form not yet defined in the first 10 years of the Web. Just as writing changed when the radio arrived, and then again when the TV arrived, it will change over time as the Web evolves into a mature media delivery system.

Your job is to learn the skills of today so that you can go out and define the style of tomorrow.

Web Sources

Andrew Sullivan: http://www.andrewsullivan.com/
BBC: http://news.bbc.co.uk/
Blogger: http://www.blogger.com/
Bloomberg News: http://www.bloomberg.com/
Cyberjournalist.net J-Blog List: http://www. cyberjournalist.net/cyberjournalists.php/
Drudge Report: http://www. drudgereport.com/
Jakob Nielsen's Web site: http://www.useit.com/
Movable Type: http://www.movabletype.org/
MSNBC: http://www.msnbc.com/
Online Journalism Review: http://www.ojr.org/
Online News Association: http://journalists.org/
Poynter Institute http://www.poynter.org/
PressThink: http://journalism.nyu.edu/pubzone/weblogs/pressthink/
The Washington Post: http://www.washingtonpost.com/

1 Locate at least three blogs on the Internet and write about a paragraph on each of them. Describe their content, their intended audience, and their style of writing. Based on your experience, write a few paragraphs that discuss your opinion on blogs as journalism. Here are a few questions to inspire your writing: Can an amateur blog be a legitimate reporter of news? Why or why not? What hazards are there for professional journalists who also publish their own blog?

2 Innovations in journalism have made Web writing the "next big thing," but what do you think? In a short paper, outline your thoughts on the transition from print and broadcast as official news sources to the ways in which the Web has gained credibility. Talk about how the Web has altered the way in which journalists look at their jobs. Is it realistic to expect writers to work in more than one form of media? Do you think a multimedia presentation enhances a story or distracts from the facts? Are you excited by the prospect of multimedia reporting, or frightened by it?

Two young girls get distracted by a video on the way toward the exit of a toy store they came to with their mothers. Originally the parents came to the store to pick up a book of Christmas toy coupons, yet the two soon realized having their daughters walk through the store was just as easy as having them look through the booklet for toys they liked. (Photograph courtesy of Amanda Goehlert.)

Converged Graphics Across All Media

We live in an increasingly visual culture. Television, the Internet, even newspapers and magazines are loaded with visual messages meant to enhance or advance journalistic storytelling. This chapter explores the ways media, such as print, broadcast, and online, use information graphics as a primary storytelling method and also discusses how convergent partnerships across media platforms can benefit from the integration of information graphics into important news coverage.

For more than 20 years, newspapers and magazines have been working to perfect the art of information graphics reporting, a craft that combines art with journalism, aesthetics, and information. Graphics reporters began to emerge in print newsrooms in the early 1980s. Newspapers took advantage of this revolution and increased the number of charts, diagrams, maps, and other visually driven story packages to help time-starved readers absorb information more quickly. These days, we have more options from which to obtain information than ever before, and the field of information graphics reporting is expanding to influence how information is presented in online and broadcast. So, while the development of the graphics reporter is generally derived from newspapers and other print publications, the skill set is beginning to translate to other mechanisms for delivering information.

Thus, when referring to the relationship between graphics and convergence, we often talk about "multimedia" graphics. Most news-oriented information graphics are developed for print, broadcast, and the Web. However, before we address how information graphics fit into the notion of media convergence, it is important to first take a look at the history of information graphics reporting and to discuss the role of the graphics reporter in a news environment.

Information Graphics History

Considered by many to be the catalyst for the information graphics explosion that began to take place in the 1980s, *USA Today* was founded in September 1982. Its editorial mission was simple: Cater to the time-starved reader with tightly edited story packages in an entertaining and easy-to-read format. This meant shorter stories, innovative use of color, and a multitude of maps, charts, polls, and other color graphics in place of the more traditional long-form, text-driven stories common in most newspapers. At *USA Today*, editors viewed information graphics as being just as effective as word-driven story structures in conveying news. As Lori Demo, a former *USA Today* editor puts it, "If the story starts to get too bogged down by explanation, it's time for a graphic." This philosophy has continued to evolve at *USA Today* for more than 20 years.

Today, most newspapers employ a number of graphics reporters who develop information graphics to enhance storytelling potential and appeal to readers in a more visual way. Print graphics come in a variety of forms, including pie, fever, and bar charts to convey statistical information, explanatory diagrams, and maps.

Information graphics also have been a common form of visual storytelling in news broadcasts for many years. Numerical displays or explanatory illustrations are often used to enhance a news broadcast by taking the viewer where video cameras cannot. In particular, maps have served an important function in broadcast news reporting for stories related to weather, politics, and war. The integration of maps into the presentation of broadcast news often enhances a viewer's ability to conceptualize and understand the importance and impact of a story. Broadcast graphics are often developed as a portion of a news story that works to complement the video and audio. The leap to these types of graphics has allowed graphics reporters to integrate animation,

82

allowing for a more realistic graphic representation of the information at hand.

As the communications power of the World Wide Web evolves, so do the formats we use to convey online news and information. News Web sites such as MSNBC.com, sun-sentinel.com (*South Florida Sun-Sentinel*), and nytimes.com (*The New York Times*) are using graphics to present information in a more visual way. Like broadcast graphics, online graphics can be animated, increasing the potential for real-time, realistic visual explanations of an event or topic. However, unlike both print and broadcast graphics, Web graphics can also be "nonlinear." In other words, given the nature of the Web, users can actually choose the order and pace in which they navigate a Web graphic, creating a much more immersive experience.

Online graphics are similar to their print and broadcast counterparts in that they generally come in the form of diagrams, charts, and maps. Interactive graphics, however, are categorized a bit more specifically. Four main types exist: *narratives*, *instructives*, *exploratives*, and *simulatives*. In 2003, Maish Nichani and Venkat Rajamanickam provided a thorough and concise definition for each. They stated that the object of a *narrative* is "to explain by giving the reader a vicarious experience of the intent through a story." In other words, a narrative involves very little interactivity and is more closely related to a broadcast graphic in that it provides a relatively passive viewing experience (see Figure 6.1). Strong narrative graphics are those that combine interesting audio voiceover with graphic depth and rich animation.

An *instructive* should "explain by enabling the reader to sequentially step through the intent." Instructive graphics are highly immersive in that they provide the reader with a chance to click through the steps of a process (see Figure 6.2). *Exploratives* "give the reader an opportunity to explore and discover the intent." Like instructives, exploratives are also highly interactive, however, the main difference is that exploratives tend to explain the subject more deeply and may include multiple graphics, audio and video clips, and photo slide shows in a single graphics package (see Figure 6.3). Exploratives are also highly nonlinear in nature. These types of interactives often include several topical points of entry, allowing readers the chance to decide in what order they will engage with the graphic's content.

Finally, *simulatives* "enable the user to experience the intent" and are usually a representation of some kind of real-word phenomena. Simulatives are also highly immersive in that they are meant to simulate

83

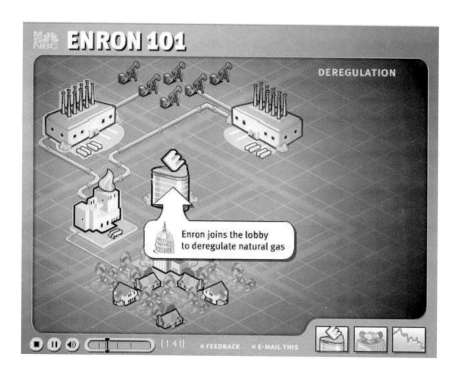

Figure 6.1 *This narrative interactive by MSNBC.com explains the rise and fall of Enron. With rich illustrations, well-paced animation, and in-depth voiceover for explanation, MSNBC.com provides a simple, easy-to-follow graphic that tells the Enron story from beginning to end. (Courtesy of MSNBC.com.)*

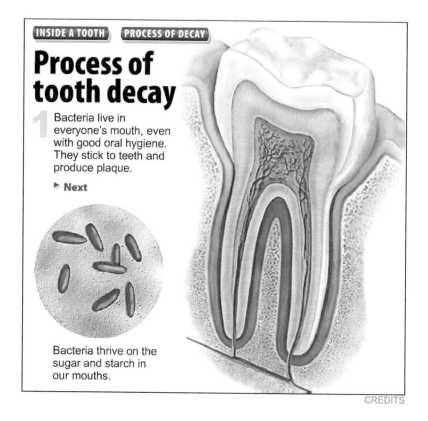

Figure 6.2 *This instructive graphic by the Sun-Sentinel provides a step-by-step explanation of how tooth decay develops. The level of interactivity is strong, allowing users to click through each step at their own pace. (Courtesy of South Florida Sun-Sentinel.)*

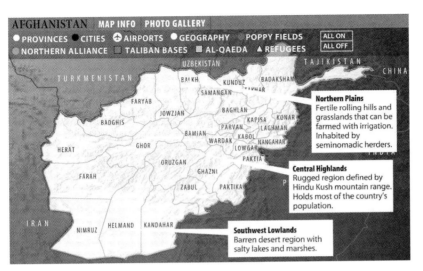

Figure 6.3 *This is an example of an explorative graphic published in 2001, by the* Sun-Sentinel. *The paper developed a series of interactives that offered a detailed look at a number of Middle Eastern countries, including Afghanistan, India, Iraq, and Iran. Each graphic included maps of the country that outlined the locations of a variety of things, as well as a photo gallery explaining key cultural facts about each country. (Courtesy of South Florida* Sun-Sentinel.)

an experience as closely as possible (see Figure 6.4). Thus, the planning process for online graphics not only includes consideration for the type of data metaphor (i.e., chart, map, or diagram), but also requires that a graphics reporter determine the actual storytelling approach for a particular set of information. The graphics reporter must also determine the most effective approach to animation and interactivity.

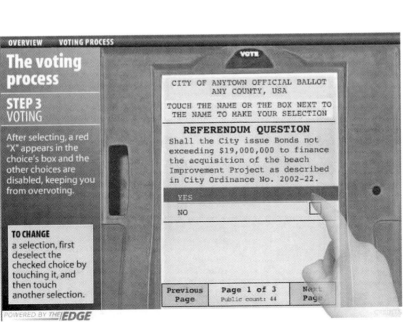

Figure 6.4 *This simulative graphic produced by the* Sun-Sentinel *allowed users a chance to practice using new voting machines adopted by Broward and Dade counties. Graphics reporters copied the appearance of the machines down to the typeface that users would see when they engaged with the real thing. (Courtesy of South Florida* Sun-Sentinel.)

Role of the Graphics Reporter

Just as a good news reporter must be capable of writing interesting stories, a strong graphics reporter must be capable of creating visually engaging illustrations. Artistic skills are extremely important to a graphics reporter's ability to create accurate, attractive graphics. However, a graphic's merit should be first judged on its ability to advance a reader's understanding of a story or event. A graphic needs to contain a clean, clear, and accurate presentation of fact-based information. A truly successful graphics reporter is a journalist first and an artist second. In other words, every artistic decision should consider the information needs of the readers, the nature of the story, and the clarity of the message.

A graphics reporter's role and responsibilities are, in many ways, similar to those of any other reporter. They engage in research for both the visual and textual elements of the graphic. They consult a variety of sources, including, but not limited to, encyclopedias, almanacs, reports, documents, and individuals who are experts in their fields. Graphics reporters often go on assignment to gather information for their work. They often attend news meetings and work with editors, photographers, and other reporters on developing story packages. They must also be accurate, observe ethical journalistic practices, and serve as credible sources of information for the audience.

However, the nature of precision differs between a reporter who uses words as the primary form of expression and one who uses information graphics. Text reporters, no matter how well they use precise and descriptive language in regard to events and scenes, are constrained by the limits of the language. A graphic has the ability to truly show what happened and how it happened. A graphics reporter can create diagrams that illustrate objects in direct proportion to their real counterparts. A graphic can show exactly "what happened," "when" and "in what order," "how much," "how close," "how far away," or "how to" in a much more conceptual fashion than words. After all, would you rather read a paragraph that describes the racial makeup of the United States by percentage, or would you rather see it in a pie chart? In this and other cases, without the visual aid, the numbers become rather meaningless because they are more difficult to process in comparison to one another. They often lack context, and, sometimes, a graphic is also a more space-efficient way to provide that information.

In a convergent environment, a graphics reporter needs to ask a second set of questions about the main points in a story and the role of graphics in telling that story. Once it has been determined what types of graphics (chart, diagram, map, etc.) are appropriate for a story, a graphics reporter must also establish how graphics will be presented using the available formats (i.e., print, online, broadcast). What parts of the graphic story are best told in print? What parts are better served online? What parts are more appropriate for broadcast? Print graphics are generally accompanied by other print elements such as photographs, headlines, and text-based stories. Print graphics are one dimensional, and the navigation is primarily determined by the design or physical organization of elements. Online graphics can be animated and allow for interactivity. They may also be accompanied by other elements such as text-based stories and still photographs, as well as video and audio clips.

However, navigation is affected by both organization of elements and the nature of the animation and interactivity. Broadcast graphics may be static, but fully animated graphics make better use of the television medium. Instead of being accompanied by text-based storytelling companions, broadcast graphics are generally integrated with video clips, reporter's notes, and audio voiceover explanations. Thus, each format has the potential to tell a portion of the story effectively and also present the graphic information in slightly different ways. Convergence, then, is best served when a graphics reporter seeks to maximize his or her storytelling potential *and* the number of people who will engage with the information by constructing graphics for a single story in multiple formats.

Cooperative efforts between newspapers and television news stations are beginning to develop information graphics in multiple media formats for a single story. Even with these partnerships, print and online graphics packages for a single story are more common. It's also important to note that most convergence efforts where information graphics are concerned develop in a single newsroom between print publications and their respective Web sites. Convergence projects involving multimedia graphics between separate news organizations are rare, partly because of the highly specialized nature of graphics reporting and the amount of time it takes to construct multimedia graphics. Yet, *The New York Times*, the *South Florida Sun-Sentinel*, *The Washington Post*, and others, frequently publish graphics for both print and the Web to support their news coverage. This often involves a cross-promotion between the print and online graphics presentations. For example, the *Sun-Sentinel* often runs full-page, stand-alone graphics in the newspaper under the reoccurring title "News Illustrated" (see Figure 6.5). When appropriate, "News Illustrated" graphics are

88

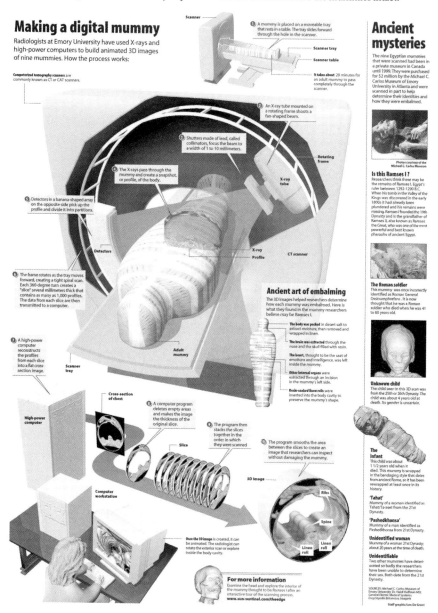

Figure 6.5 Sun-Sentinel *"News Illustrated" graphics like this one range in topic from science and technology to the war on terror. When an interactive graphic is also available for viewing online, the print graphic refers readers to the Web site to learn more about the topic. (Courtesy of South Florida Sun-Sentinel.)*

accompanied by interactive graphics presented on the paper's online interactive graphics gallery called, "The Edge" (see http://www.sun-sentinel.com/broadband/theedge). When a "News Illustrated" graphic runs in the paper, readers are encouraged to visit the Web site to see the related multimedia graphic (see Figure 6.6). According to *Sun-Sentinel* graphics director Don Wittekind, most of the multimedia efforts at the paper are extensions of major print projects. "While multimedia was once an afterthought, it's now discussed seriously in the earliest planning meetings," he says. "This has actually raised my department's stress level a little, because where I once judged each project and decided whether I wanted to get graphics involved, I no longer have that option. I can now expect the managing editor to turn to me and say, 'So what are we doing for the multimedia component?'"

One Story, Multiple Graphics

The field of information graphics reporting is still pretty strongly rooted in newspaper newsrooms. Most television stations still don't include graphics departments in the newsroom, and few online staffs have individuals whose sole responsibility is graphics reporting. Graphics reporters employed by the newspaper produce most multimedia

89

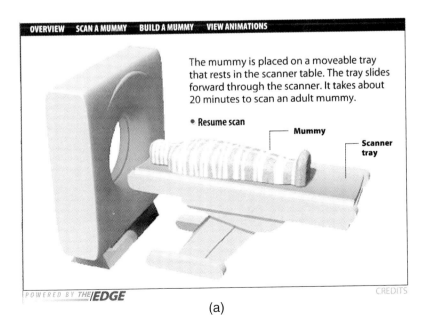

(a)

Figure 6.6 *Graphics published on the* Sun-Sentinel's *interactive gallery, "The Edge," often contain similar information to that of the print graphics. However, due to the nature of the Web, online graphics can often go where print cannot. This multilayered graphic allows a user (a) to explore the mummy scanning process and (b) to see animations of the external and internal portions of a mummy. (Courtesy of South Florida* Sun-Sentinel.)

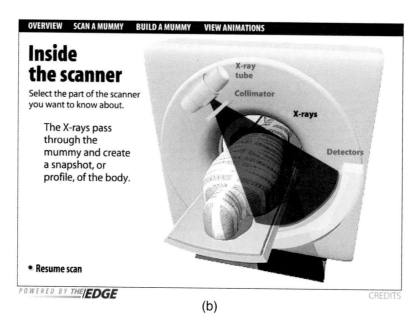

OVERVIEW   SCAN A MUMMY   BUILD A MUMMY   VIEW ANIMATIONS

Inside
the scanner

Select the part of the scanner
you want to know about.

The X-rays pass
through the
mummy and create
a snapshot, or
profile, of the body.

X-ray
tube

Collimator

X-rays

Detectors

• Resume scan

POWERED BY *THE* **/EDGE**

CREDITS

Figure 6.6 *Cont'd.*   (b)

90

graphics packages. At the *Sun-Sentinel*, for example, a relatively large staff of graphics reporters is trained to use a variety of software programs, including Macromedia FreeHand (illustration), Macromedia Flash (animation), and Newtek Lightwave (3D).

Challenges and considerations are associated with each format. Due to the linear nature of print, all of the content must fit into a single space. Without the potential for motion or sound, print graphics reporters must find innovative ways to convey movement and action. Graphics reporters are often limited by the space available for a graphic in newspapers. However, on the bright side, print graphics can generally be produced more quickly than those created for other media. Space is virtually unlimited on the Web, and because the Web is non-linear, you can present the information in multiple, separate scenes or steps. Add to that the ability to integrate audio, video, text, and interactivity, and online graphics can be an incredibly rich, immersive experience for audiences. Broadcast graphics often integrate animation, video, and audio and can provide viewers with a much more realistic portrayal of events. But broadcast news is generally presented in very short, 1- to 2-minute clips. Thus, a broadcast graphic must convey a point in about 20 to 30 seconds.

So, how does a multimedia graphics package come together? The answer to this question really depends on the nature of the partnership. In some cases, reporters from each publication/broadcast work together to develop the story and gather reference materials. A text-based and/or graphics reporter from the newspaper, a field reporter or videographer from the television station, and a producer from the Web site might work together to conceptualize the entire story package. However, when it comes to the creation of the graphics for all three formats, it's usually more efficient for the same graphics reporter or team of graphics reporters to develop them all. That's because the main illustrations and much of the key information will be shared among all of the graphics.

Graphics reporters at the *Sun-Sentinel* often develop graphics for both the newspaper and the Web site. Occasionally, they also produce broadcast graphics intended for use by a broadcast "news partner." Although Tribune Co., the media conglomerate that owns the *Sun-Sentinel*, doesn't own a broadcast station in Ft. Lauderdale, this doesn't stop the paper from collaborating with broadcast journalists. In 2002, for example, *Sun-Sentinel* graphics reporters successfully created three graphics packages to cover a single local news story. When Florida officials tried to sink a decommissioned Navy ship, called the *Spiegel Grove*, to construct an artificial reef off the coast of south Florida, a mishap left the 5,000-ton vessel upside-down and sticking out of the water for more than a week. In a collaborative effort with CBS Channel 4 News (WFOR), graphics reporters at the *Sun-Sentinel* covered the story by developing information graphics for print, the Web, and broadcast. *Sun-Sentinel* graphics director Don Wittekind said a team-based approach was adopted for this project. Graphics were designed to show how a salvage company brought in to properly resink the vessel was planning to accomplish its goal (see Figure 6.7).

The team consisted of five people, each in charge of one of the following responsibilities: research and reporting and print page production, 3D modeling of the *Spiegel Grove*, 3D animation of the 3D *Spiegel Grove* model, Web design for online animation, and video production and special effects for broadcast. The team started by getting the graphics reporter to research the salvage company, while the 3D artist worked on the model of the ship, Wittekind explained. As soon as the model was roughed out, a copy was given to the animator and a rendering was made for the print product. Although these were not finished images, they were complete enough to allow work to continue on three fronts.

92

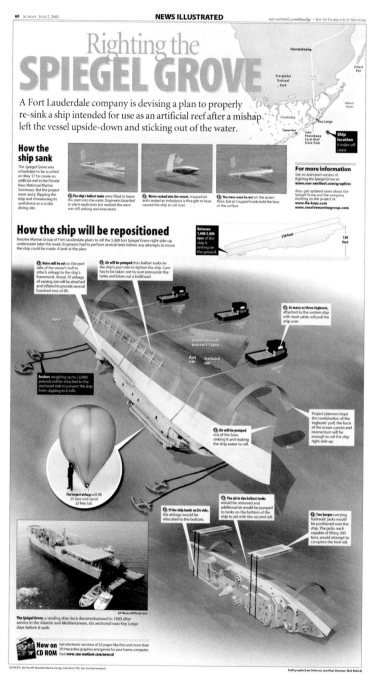

Figure 6.7 *When the Spiegel Grove story broke, a team of graphics reporters at the* Sun-Sentinel *began working diligently to develop a convergent graphics package that included a component for (a) print, (b) online, and (c) broadcast. (Courtesy of South Florida Sun-Sentinel.)*

(a)

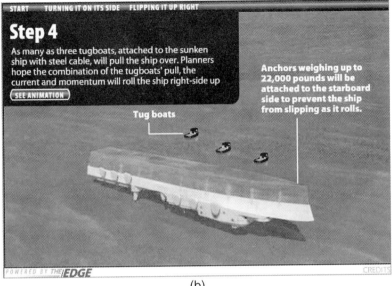

(b)

(c)

93

Figure 6.7 *Cont'd.*

Once the text was finalized, this was given to the Web designer, along with multiple renderings of the ship, to allow him to work on the online animation. When the final illustration of the ship was ready, they were able to place it on the print page and into the Web animation. For broadcast, the animation was done with an early model of the ship, so reporters only had to update the model and render out the animation. The final step was to take the broadcast illustration into After Effects to add the final touches and special effects.

By making sure that everyone was able to work on the project simultaneously, all three components were ready for publication on the same day. The *Spiegel Grove* project is a fine example of how information graphics can provide a convergence partnership with an amazing array of resources for readers/viewers/Web users looking for thorough coverage of a single topic.

The Power of Information Graphics

It is important for all journalists to understand the significance and power of information graphics in news coverage. Not everyone will possess the highly specialized skills needed for creating the graphics. However, reporters, producers, editors, and photographers alike must be able to recognize when a graphic is necessary as well as conceptualize a graphic within a story package. Look for visual cues within a story and propose a graphic when the answers to the questions "who," "what," "when," "where," "why," or "how" are visual. Sometimes this means paying close attention as a reporter or editor is describing the story at hand, always listening for words, phrases, and concepts that suggest a graphic.

Work to simplify complicated information. Specific numbers, visual descriptions of objects or events, and identifiable locations don't always jump out, and a graphic may not always present itself right away. A good journalist will often discover a graphic's potential in less obvious ways. Is the explanation in a story getting bogged down and difficult to follow? If so, can the information be organized in a more graphic way? Is there information that can be conveyed conceptually to put a thought or idea into a more visual perspective? Using visual metaphors (or "data metaphors" in the case of mathematical or quantifiable information) is often a simpler way for people to digest information.

Look for comparisons, dates, or other organizational facts outlined in the story. Who are the key players and why? What are the key dates? How did we get here? Where do we go from here? What's at issue, and what does it mean for the reader? These types of questions often lead to discovering graphic potential within a story, and by presenting the answers in a graphic manner, you provide readers with a quickly accessible and easily understood context for the rest of the story.

Finally, once it has been determined that a graphic is needed, begin conceptualizing what form the graphic should take as well how the graphic might change across two or three platforms. If it's a print graphic, you'll need to be conscious of how much space is available, and you'll need to keep in mind that all of the information will be presented in one space, all together. When developing the graphic for the Web, you'll want to consider which type of interactive—narrative, instructive, explorative, or simulative—will be the most effective way of conveying the information. What form will be most helpful in the audience's efforts to understand the information at hand? How will animation and interactivity affect a user's navigation of the content? Finally, if you're also developing a graphic for broadcast, you must figure out how to synthesize the information into 20 to 30 seconds. How will the script for the audio explanation read? How will animation and pace affect understanding?

Given the time and talent it takes to develop information graphics for any medium, finding the answers to these questions isn't always easy. Depending on the nature of the story and the time frame of the deadline, the creation of graphics for any format could take any-where from a few hours to a few weeks. Information graphics are an extremely powerful storytelling method for all kinds of journalists. They often take us where cameras or reporters cannot. They simplify complicated information by giving it a visual context, capitalizing on the fact that most people tend to understand better when text *and* images are combined. As they make their way across multiple media platforms, information graphics can optimize the number of people who not only encounter the information, but possibly the number of people who engage with more than one media outlet. As advances in technology, such as faster Internet connections and better 3D and animation software, continue to occur, the storytelling potential of information graphics reporters is becoming limitless.

References

Nichani, M., & Rajamanickam, V. (2003, September). *Interactive visual explainers—A simple classification.* Retrieved October 14, 2004, from http://www.elearningpost.com/features/archives/002069.asp

95

1 In your favorite newspaper or magazine, search for a story that is driven by visual explanations. Then, conceptualize how you might develop three separate but interrelated graphics packages—one for print, one for the Web, and one for broadcast—for a number of converged media outlets. Consider what parts of the story would be better served in print. What parts would benefit from interactivity and nonlinear organization? What portions would combine well with video and animation? Then, consider how the packages could support and refer to one another. Finally, sketch some ideas for how each graphics package would look. Keep in mind that the print graphic would all be organized in a single space; that a Web graphic would include some degree of interactivity; and that a broadcast graphic would be strongest if it included animation and audio voiceovers to provide explanations.

2 Using the sketches from Exercise 1, conduct some research for your graphics, and write the text blocks that will accompany any illustration. Remember that the text for a print graphic will all be presented in the same general space and should be written concisely in order to conserve space. Additionally, think about how interactive navigation and the segmentation of content affects how text is written for a Web graphic. Finally, if your broadcast graphic contains verbal explanations, it must come in the form of audio. So, you are writing a script that will accompany the broadcast graphic, and pace and tone are key considerations.

A golfer lines up his putt after setting his cigar on the green during the 47th Mad Anthony's Celebrity Pro-Am tournament held at Sycamore Hills Golf Club on June 21 in Fort Wayne, Indiana. (Photograph courtesy of Will Vragovic.)

Digital Still Photography

Kenny Irby of the Poynter Institute defines photojournalism as the craft of employing photographic storytelling to document life. It is universal and transcends cultural and language boundaries.

Photojournalism is not restricted to still pictures or film cameras or any location. Photojournalism tells stories about life. Sometimes those stories can be held in the hands to be examined in detail. Sometimes the stories flicker across a television screen at 30 frames per second. Sometimes the stories are organized online and can be explored by the viewer.

However presented, the basis for good photojournalism comes from news judgment and reporting skills employed by the storyteller. We have been storytellers since the first human beings began to describe their surroundings. They were interested in the news of the day. Where is the food? Is there better shelter? We've been using pictures to tell and enhance the stories for thousands of years.

The Power of the Still Photograph

The demise of still photojournalism has been forecast for decades, but nothing matches the power of that well-chosen frozen moment in time.

Video often shows an event to a passive audience. The viewer sits and watches as the scene unfolds. Still photographs can be examined fleetingly or in detail.

In most cases, the viewer of a still photograph is in control. The viewer decides how long to look and where to focus attention. This gives power to the viewer, power to the photograph, and power to the photographer. The skillful photographer directs attention to the key elements in a picture but how the image is seen ultimately rests with the viewer.

Still photographs appear to have a sense of permanence. One moment selected out of the parade of images that fly past the lens is captured, selected, and immortalized. Video achieves its power through the very impermanence of its images. The images fly by, propelling the viewer through the story at the pace set by the editor. The story can be recorded and watched multiple times, but the relationship to the images is different. Collectively, the video images form a whole and do not usually stand on their own as individual pictures.

The challenge in a converged media environment is to take advantage of the power of all media. Use the power of the still image with its seeming permanence, but also harness sound and the energy of motion. Multimedia presentations have the potential to harness the power from both of these types of imagery. In a converged environment, the picture editor's role, already important in any single medium, becomes even more important.

Issues such as how to frame an image and shot composition are covered elsewhere in this book. This chapter outlines the history and the technology associated with photojournalism as well as the ways in which to select and display images based on the medium with which you are working. The purpose is to serve as an opening gambit for future discussions that will refine and expand the discussion of how to use images to tell stories across media platforms.

Impact of Technology on Photographic Reporting

In 1855, barely a decade and a half after photography came into public knowledge, Roger Fenton, the first war photographer to make surviving images, and his assistant Marcus Sparling traveled through the Crimea with state-of-the-art equipment. Fenton brought two servants, three horses, a photographic wagon about the size of a small motor home

Figure 7.1 *Marcus Sparling is shown seated on Roger Fenton's photography van. The pair spent four months in the Crimea and captured approximately 300 images of the war immortalized in Tennyson's* Charge of the Light Brigade *(Photograph courtesy of the U.S. Library of Congress, Prints & Photographs Division.)*

101

(see Figure 7.1), 36 large cases of equipment, five cameras, and 700 glass plates.

Fenton was there to document the war that many of you know of through the poem, *The Charge of the Light Brigade* by Tennyson. His approach to his work was influenced by the technology of his time. The collodion process that he used for making his negatives required that the plates be exposed before the emulsion dried out, a difficult challenge in the hot spring and summer weather.

Many of the exposures took half a minute or more, so action pictures were not possible. Making matters worse, the van itself became an attractive target for Russian artillery. Fenton narrowly escaped injury once when the roof was blown from the wagon and again while setting up one of the cameras.

Fenton, like his American Civil War counterparts organized by Matthew Brady (see Figure 7.2), was relying on direct distribution of

Figure 7.2 *Images from the Civil War era, like this one, were often taken well after an event had concluded. Action shots were impossible because it took half an hour or more to capture a single frame. (Photograph courtesy of the U.S. Library of Congress, Prints & Photographs Division.)*

102

his pictures because newspapers and magazines of the time had no way of directly printing a photograph.

The Democratization of Photography

George Eastman's company, Kodak, introduced film on a flexible roll, and you can probably see how this was a big improvement over the single-image glass plates. The snapshot cameras introduced in 1888 would allow 100 pictures to be made on a single roll of film.

Eastman's marketing plan, based on the slogan "You press the button, we do the rest," had another impact on visual communication. Virtually anyone, anywhere, was now able to make pictures. This "democratization of photography" led to the beginnings of our more visually oriented society by helping to create a more visually literate audience.

About this same time, social reformers discovered the power of the photograph. Jacob Riis, a reporter for the New York *Evening Sun* who exposed the plight of new immigrants in the 1880s and 1890s, and Lewis Hine, a crusader against child labor a quarter century later, employed pictures to put a face on these issues. Hine used information about the children's health, size, and age along with notes from their conversations to give greater emphasis to the pictures (see Figure 7.3).

(a)

(b)

Figure 7.3 *Lewis Hine used images like (a) this young shrimp and oyster worker in Biloxi, Mississippi, and (b) this boy sweeper at a cotton mill in Evansville, Indiana, to put a face on child labor in the early 1900s. (Photographs courtesy of the U.S. Library of Congress, Prints & Photographs Division.)*

You might say that he was one of the first to use the techniques of converged media as they are used today.

The Birth of Modern Photojournalism

The 1930s brought what is termed by some as "the birth of modern photojournalism." Technological advances included flexible gelatin film for press cameras; the advent of the smaller "Speed Graphic" camera, which replaced its larger predecessors; flash bulbs that could be synchronized with the shutter of the camera allowing sports action photography; the adoption of the 35-mm camera for some types of candid photography; the first practical color films; the wire-transmission of pictures over the networks of the Associated Press and United Press; the advent of the picture magazine in Europe; and the beginnings of documentary photography through the Depression Era's Farm Security Administration.

Significant technological advancements of the 1950s included the beginnings of the widespread adoption of 35-mm cameras, the introduction of medium-grained high-speed film, and the introduction of the electronic flash. By the 1960s and into the 1970s, television was well on its way to becoming a dominant force in mass media. Its impact was being felt in the newspaper and magazine newsrooms of America. The major, general-interest picture magazines were on their way out. Newspapers were beginning to use color regularly and were adopting the candid, documentary approach of those magazines for news and feature coverage with coordinated picture stories. Technological advancement in still photography was mainly in improvements to lenses and films as well as the introduction of computerization and miniaturization.

The Digital Age

During the 1980s, Sony, Canon, and Nikon worked to perfect still-video cameras. *USA Today* published pictures from the presidential nominating conventions in 1988 using still-video technology and digital systems soon followed.

The first digital cameras cost tens of thousands of dollars and had poor resolution. Adoption of digital camera technology didn't really begin until the late 1990s. However, the adoption of digital cameras was rapid, and by the beginning of the 21st century, most newspapers had moved into digital photography.

Today's journalists still term the equipment bulky, but compare Roger Fenton's wagonload of "state-of-the-art" equipment in 1855 to the *Dallas Morning News'* Cheryl Diaz Meyer's equipment for her trip to Afghanistan about 150 years later. She carried two Nikon D1 H camera bodies, a 17–35-mm lens, a 60-mm lens, an 80–200-mm lens, an electronic flash, eight camera batteries, two camera battery chargers, 50 AA batteries, an AC power adapter, 15 memory cards, a laptop computer, two laptop batteries, a DC power adapter, a power strip, and a high-speed satellite video phone. All totaled, she carried about 100 pounds of photography and computer equipment and another 100 pounds of satellite telephone equipment.

Fenton brought back approximately 300 pictures from his four months in the Crimea. They were offered for sale to the public six to eight months after they were made. Meyer was able to transmit 15 or more pictures a day. All were ready for newspaper publication the day that they were made. She was also able to set up a high-speed connection to the Internet to stay abreast of the news as it unfolded.

The technological advances in a century and a half would astound the pioneers. Even with all of that change, the goal has remained the same. Photojournalists want to tell the story the way that they saw it and get it to their audience quickly and faithfully. The methods and the tools have changed, but the ideal remains.

Picture Editing for Different Media

The roles of editor and photographer are interdependent. A good editor improves good work and makes excellent material sparkle. To be most successful, the collaboration must begin before a single picture is made. Photographer, reporter, and editor should meet and discuss plans for the story at the proposal stage. Planning is the key to successful projects. The editor's role is to challenge and to question the story: What's this story about? How are you going to tell the story? What have you left out? Where are the redundancies?

The effective editor is the "gatekeeper" for the story and has the keys to the information. A good story is tightly edited with a beginning, middle, and end. It is constructed like a house of cards. If one of the cards is removed, the house falls; if another is added, the weight of redundancy also brings it down.

105

The tightest edits are usually for newspaper layouts. In this format, sometimes a single image must tell the story. Getting down to that single image often involves a number of difficult decisions, including what story the image must tell and how well the image matches with a written story that might accompany it. When more than one image is needed, the pictures are edited and displayed in a spatial relationship to one another. The most important picture in terms of storytelling often is the one that dominates the others in size and placement. That key image will likely be one and a half to twice the size of the next largest picture. Dominant pictures usually work best on the top half of a page. Visual elements, pictures, headlines, and graphics should be grouped in an effective manner with any white space to the outside. All of these elements have a spatial relationship with one another. Broadsheet newspaper picture pages are usually most effective with five or fewer pictures with or without text.

Magazine layouts can be spatial and relational, but they can also be organized in a linear way over several pages. Effective magazine presentation works like the newspaper layout, but on a smaller scale, with the pictures strung together and each dominating a spread in the magazine.

Effective Web site design can draw on newspaper and magazine styles of layout, but it can also look to other media for innovation as the producers try to transmit the stories in the most effective way. Slideshow options are often available to Web photographers, and these options allow for the images to be viewed one at a time. The storytelling premises discussed earlier still remain important, because the slideshow should move the reader from image to image with a purpose. Simply throwing a handful of photos into a slideshow does little to help users understand the value in what they are seeing.

Movie and video edits are linear. They progress frame by frame, scene by scene, and sequence by sequence. Still pictures can be used effectively if they are edited and organized like a movie or video production. Look to Chapters 8 and 9 of this book for more information about shooting and editing for video.

Ken Burns may be the best-known producer of documentary films working today. He makes extensive use of historical still pictures. Take a look at his Civil War documentary and examine the way in which the pictures are organized to tell the stories. Multimedia producers either online or in digital media formats can build on Burns's techniques. The stories usually move in a linear fashion, but can employ spatial techniques to highlight key moments or information. Multi-media picture editing is in its infancy, but producers can draw on the past. From the 1960s through the 1980s, photographers produced a variety of multiple-projector slide-tape shows. Creative individuals and teams produced shows that created a mosaic of images, timed to music and narration. It's much easier to get the same effects today by using computer software and digital images.

One aspect of multimedia production that eludes the other media is the ability of the producers to add interactivity to the production. The editor still retains the gatekeeper function but allows the viewer to access it in more than one way. For example, in a series of stories about political candidates, the stories could be organized so that each candidate's full story is presented from start to finish: education, experience, religious background, views, or any number of issues, and so on. Click on candidate A and get the full story, then click on candidate B and continue until you have covered all of the candidates. Another way to access the information could be to look at all the educational backgrounds of all candidates one by one and then move on to looking at their religious backgrounds. Images, video clips, and other material can also be viewed in this nonlinear fashion.

Photographers' Responsibilities for Different Media

The reason for discussing the editing before we discussed the photography is that the photographer must approach the image acquisition differently based on the intended outcome. To photograph for a print product, the photographer must create a story in a limited number of images. Space in print is always at a premium. Tight edits and a few outstanding pictures carry the day in print media. The photographer must make sure that each picture is top quality and that the four or five pictures used on a page provide all of the information needed to convey the full story.

If the pictures are to be used in a video production or in a multimedia format, the constraint of numbers is lessened. A linear picture story contains pictures that may be redundant in message, but because of the way that the production progresses from picture to picture at a set speed, producers use that repetition to build up the importance of that piece of information.

If the photographer is unsure of the intended final use of a set of pictures, then he or she must shoot for the broadest edit. All of the bases must be covered in a variety of ways. Shooting still pictures for linear stories is a bit like shooting for video in that there should be different views of the same subject so that the editor can create the visual variety needed to make the production interesting.

Here is an example that might help to illustrate what we mean. In television news, you'll notice that when the camera moves from one view of a person to another view of that same person, you sometimes see an intervening shot called a "cutaway." The camera might start with a tight profile shot of a speaker. The editor wants use a shot of the same speaker from head-on to get a good look at a dramatic hand gesture. The editor will usually select a transitional shot like a member of the audience listening before the camera cuts to the new view of the speaker. Still photographers who work in multimedia or shoot for Web site products must also get into the habit of shooting transitions.

A good exercise for photographers and editors to help them in the planning stages of their projects is to make a storyboard of the shots or the concepts that must be included in the final presentation. A storyboard is simply a sketchbook of the planned story. Works of fiction like movies are heavily storyboarded. Every scene and most shots are sketched out in advance.

To better understand how storyboards work, take a look at the construction and organization of a good graphic novel or a comic book. The story text flows from scene to scene, but the artists use a variety of cinematic effects to enhance the story. Good photographers also use a variety of shots and perspectives to move their stories along. Wide shots, close-ups, detail shots, medium shots, and portraits all work together to visually tell the story in an interesting fashion. If all of the pictures look the same, it does not matter that the content is different. The viewer will get bored and move on to something else.

News photographers who shoot still images use a modified storyboard technique called the "throw down." The photographer makes a broad rough edit that includes different pictures that have similar information into work-prints or computer printouts and spreads them out on a table or on the floor. Then the editing team goes through the story concept by concept and point by point to select the best package of pictures to tell the story. Sometimes an excellent picture will not make the final cut because it is redundant or there is another lesser picture that makes the whole stronger.

Conflicting Ethical Standards among Media Outlets

One thing to bear in mind is the standard of ethical behavior for a particular medium. Just because the storyboard calls for a particular picture does not mean that the journalist should go out and create that image. Photojournalists should tell a story that reflects what actually happened.

Print photojournalists usually adhere to a standard of minimal interference. Historians of journalism ethics will tell you that this is a position that has evolved over time. The grandfather of the picture story, W. Eugene Smith, maintained that he adhered to the truth in his pictures, but truth is a flexible concept. Smith was known to combine images from different negatives to add "truthful" symbolism to a picture. Smith once said: "I am constantly torn between the attitude of the conscientious journalist who is a recorder and interpreter of the facts and of the creative artist who often is necessarily at poetic odds with the literal facts." One example is a famous photograph of Dr. Albert Schweitzer in which Smith inserted the images from different negatives of a saw and a reaching hand to add to what he saw as the "truth" of the statement of the picture. Such manipulation of still pictures today is usually grounds for dismissal from a news publication. Most news publications expect pictures they publish to represent what the photographer saw through the viewfinder when the picture was made. Fact and fair representation are the goals of most mainstream print journalists today.

This same "hands-off" standard does not always hold in video news packages. Frequently, when television news interviews are being shot with one camera, the shots of the interviewer are made after the interview has been completed. Video needs those cutaway shots to maintain continuity in its linear format. The interviewer usually sits and nods or looks thoughtful and those pictures are intercut with answers from the interview. Occasionally, the interviewer is photographed asking questions at a time different from the actual questioning of the subject. The questions are the same, with the only difference being the timing and the direction of the camera.

109

Positive and Negative Aspects of the Multiple-Medium Photographer

A growing number of still photojournalists are either going into video photography full time or are augmenting their still coverage with video. Technological advances, mainly in the reduction in size of broadcast-quality digital cameras, have made it feasible for a single photographer to carry still equipment and video equipment to a shoot.

One of the first well-known still photojournalists to switch to video was two-time Pulitzer Prize winner Stanley Foreman. He ended a newspaper career at the *Boston Herald-American* and began working for television. For most photojournalists, the switch is more gradual. Newspapers across the country have video components attached to their Web sites. Content must come from somewhere. David Leeson of the *Dallas Morning News* has been a newspaper photojournalist for more than a quarter century. Since late in 2000, he has been a full-time "digital video photojournalist." He asserts that the photographer of the future will no longer use still cameras, but will photograph everything with high-resolution digital video (DV).

Photojournalism veteran Dirk Halstead of *Time* and Tom Burton of the *Orlando Sentinel* invented the term *platypus* for the new breed of DV photojournalist. The metaphor of the creature that looked like it was put together from parts of birds and mammals is apt for a multifunctional role that combines the skill of still photography with animation, audio, and video production. Halstead has run DV workshops since 1999 advocating a documentary style of video photojournalism that is heavily dependent on the structures and styles of still photojournalism.

Editors who made selections from tens of pictures in the middle of the 20th century, and hundreds of images in the still digital age, will have tens of thousands of possible selections when resolution in digital video matches that of still cameras. They also will have the option of running the video on the Web site or co-owned television station.

One problem with one photographer trying to make images for more than one outlet is the conflict between capturing that frozen fraction of a second and fulfilling the basic needs of broadcast news. Still images are dependent on that iconographic key moment that tells the complete story. If the photographer is looking away trying to get a cutaway shot for the video report, the decisive moment might be missed.

110

Video organization and still organization are different. The field of DV or "platypus" journalism is still in its infancy. How the field will continue to evolve is still in question. One thing to consider is that the current storytelling forms are different for video and still stories.

Look at how *Sports Illustrated* covers an event. With long lenses, their photojournalists capture the feral look in the athlete's eye as they close in on the player's sweat-drenched, tightly framed face. Compare that to the way the television covers the same event. Most of the shots are far wider. When was the last time you saw live television coverage of a game that showed those close moments that the *SI* audience treasures? NFL films approach the intimate drama with their documentaries. They employ high-speed cameras and playback in slow motion. They can intercut tight shots that don't have a place in the live coverage.

One thing is clear. The role of the picture editor will become ever more important. More images mean more skill and work to organize those images to tell stories. Still images or video images or whatever might come next will require a strong hand to organize the photographers and a strong eye to organize the content.

Regardless of the source, still images retain their power of freezing moments in time. That power frequently transcends the power of the moving image. Still images will be key elements in the storytelling process for journalists and others into the future. There will be a place for still photography side by side with motion photography until a new medium exists that can combine the strengths of both.

Web Sources

Examples of good photojournalism, both still and video: http://www.nppa.org/competitions/

Hypertext version of Jacob Riis's book *How the Other Half Lives*: http://www.yale.edu/amstud/inforev/riis/title.html

Information on the Farm Security Administration: http://memory.loc.gov/ammem/fsowhome.html

Information on Dirk Halstead's advocacy for digital video journalism: http://www.digitaljournalist.org/

Information on Roger Fenton: http://www.loc.gov/rr/print/coll/251_fen.html

Information on the giants of photojournalism: http://www.masters-of-photography.com/index.html

Photography history from Kodak: http://www.kodak.com/US/en/corp/kodakHistory/index.shtml

111

1 Find and watch a Ken Burns documentary or other photography-based documentary. In a short paper, talk a bit about what images were used and how they helped bring meaning to the piece. Also, deconstruct the use of still pictures in part of a Burns documentary. How were the photographs used to tell a story? What did the producers and editors do to augment the images? What about the photographs made them valuable?

2 Find an event that is happening in your area and photograph it. Make copies of your images and conduct a storyboarding or "throw down" with them. When you've selected the images you think tell the story best, sketch out a plan as to how they would be displayed in a newspaper, magazine, and on the Web. Also, write a short paper that explains what you did, how you did it, and why you've arrived at this result.

The Beneficence statue on the Ball State University campus stands glazed with ice topped by snow that fell during the January 2005 ice storm which left a half inch of ice on trees and tens of thousands of residents without power. (Photograph courtesy of Amanda Goehlert.)

Digital Video Photography

Photography means "writing with light." The words come from the Greek words for "light" (*photo*) and "writing" (*graphus*). Regardless of what you call what you do—photojournalism, videography, or photography—it is all photography and it all involves writing with light. We acquire our images with a variety of tools, but it requires light to reflect off of our subject for us to see them. As photojournalists we use light as our medium to tell stories. In this chapter you will learn the basics of digital video photography to tell stories for television and the Web.

The Professional Television Camera

Every camera has a few basic parts, starting with a light-tight box. You may be shooting on film, or using a charged coupled device (CCD)—known as a chip—to capture the image. Regardless of the medium on which the camera records, it needs to do so in a controlled environment so that light does not enter.

The camera also needs a lens. Most television cameras use a variable focal length lens, more commonly known as a zoom lens. This allows photographers the liberty of many different focal lengths without having to carry a case full of lenses.

Every camera needs to have some type of imaging device. Most cameras these days use a CCD. The CCD owes its heritage to film and the vacuum imaging tube. The camera's electronics convert the light to digital information. The ones and zeros can then be recorded on tape, disc, or some other memory storage device.

Beyond the basic parts, the camera has numerous controls that can be used to optimize the image and adjusted to each user's preferences. No matter what camera you use, it's vital you become familiar with its operation. A good photographer can adjust the camera without looking at the buttons and switches.

White and Black Balancing

You need to be able to adjust the exposure and focus in addition to both white and black balancing the camera. A white balance is how the camera adjusts for different types of light. If you tell the camera what white is, all of the other colors will fall correctly into place. First you need to select the correct filter for the type of light at the scene. Often, position 1 on the filter wheel is no filter and is used for indoor or tungsten light at 3,200 degrees kelvin. Position 3 is usually selected for outdoors under daylight at about 5,600 degrees kelvin. You want to make sure that you manually white balance (and not rely on the automatic white-balance feature many cameras have) before you begin to shoot. If you fail to get a correct white balance, your images may appear to be blue or reddish. Either way, it's not the natural look you want for news coverage.

To set the white balance on most cameras, you aim the camera at a white object in the same location and lighting as your subject, and press a switch momentarily. In the field, reporters typically would use a piece of white printer paper or a page from a notebook. The camera will automatically adjust and often tell you the exact color temperature of the light reflecting off the white. Many cameras also have a factory preset white balance that is useful for most situations such as natural daylight or artificial light.

A black balance is similar, except that it should be performed before you white balance. The black balance establishes a correct output level for the camera. You don't need to find a black object because the camera automatically closes the lens aperture and sets its own black balance.

Composing Images for the Screen, Television, and Computer

You want the images you capture to be as pleasing as possible. For news photography, they should also look natural. You want viewers to feel as though they were at the scene. At the same time, you want to show them something they wouldn't have noticed if they were there.

Photographic composition follows the same rules established for paintings and drawings. Every frame of video should be able to stand on its own as far as composition is concerned. Shoot from the perspective that you should be able to hang every image on the wall or even make a postcard from your frames.

Framing and Composing

117

You should usually avoid placing the subject in the center of the frame. People read left to right, so their eyes are conditioned to naturally go to a point about two-thirds up the page. The same conditioning works when you are looking at a video screen. The rule of thirds is one of the most useful tools of composition. If you divide the television screen into three equal parts both horizontally and vertically, your main subject should appear on those lines and at the intersections of those lines. Think of it as a tic-tac-toe grid on the screen. Place the skyline or horizon on either the top or bottom line of the upper third. That will give you either more sky or less sky depending on your subject. Place people on the left or right third line with the balance of space providing looking room. Avoid having your subject looking at the edge of the screen or about to exit the frame.

A dominant foreground with related background and its opposite of a dominant background with related foreground are both good composition techniques. Some good examples include a low-angle shot of a football on the ground as the game is played in the field behind, or the weathered hands of an artist molding a spinning mound of clay while he sits in the background, looking at his work.

Certain subjects and locations call for certain composition. A long, straight railroad track can lead you to your subject. Rows of stacked wood can draw your eyes to the end where a man is hard at work sawing.

Balance the subject with his or her environment. Your compositions should enhance—not distract from—the subject and scene.

A level horizon is important in news photography. It may be unnatural, but a crooked shot can give the suggestion of a slanted or biased view of your subject. Leave the cock-eyed views to Hollywood and people's home movies.

Shooting Sequences: The Basis for Good Storytelling

Because we want the audience to be able to experience the scene as if they were there, we need to try to imitate the way our minds process a scene. The best way for us to do that is to use sequences.

A sequence is a series of shots that when edited together tell a story. A sequence can be as few as two shots or as many as you can imagine. Typically, we think of a three- to four-shot sequence as being wide, medium, close-up, and extreme close-up shots. The shots follow a natural progression of how our minds process visual information.

When you walk into a room, you first see a wide shot of the whole scene. It establishes where you are and what you are going to be seeing next. As you move farther into the room, you see the subjects in a medium shot. You capture more and more detail as you get a better view of the action in the scene.

You concentrate on what the subject is doing with a close-up shot. Even more detail is visible as you look very closely with an extreme close-up shot that lets you determine exactly what is happening in the room. The mind acts as both camera and editor, following the action and the reaction. That same process is what you want to imitate when you shoot and edit the story.

The Human Eye Does not Zoom or Pan

Notice when you entered the room that you didn't immediately move your body straight to the action. You processed each area in separate shots. You also didn't move your head from one side of the room to the other watching every detail along the way. The eye and the mind work together to cut to the action and the reaction. You should try to shoot your sequences in a natural progression that does not use zooms or pans.

Even a rack focus, focusing on one object then adjusting the focus to another while recording the scene, is unnatural. Try this: Hold your finger 3 to 4 inches in front of your face. Concentrate on your finger, then immediately look beyond your finger to something far away from you. Your eye changes focus from your finger to the far subject in an instant. It is a cut, not a rack focus, and thus it is best for you to rely on cuts as much as possible.

You also want to avoid using camera moves when shooting for the Web. Video is compressed for the Web to transfer at a lower bandwidth. The more a scene or shot changes, the more computer memory is used to process the scene using a compression formula and, hence, the slower the images will play for the audience.

Shooting by sequences also gives you more control over the pacing and timing of your story. You may shoot a subject performing a task that takes 30 seconds to complete in real time. With a good sequence, you might be able to compress the time into 10 seconds or even expand the time to make it last 45 seconds. Editing depends on the tone you are trying to create. You probably would not want a fast-paced quickly edited sequence for a funeral scene. Using sequences to tell a story gives you the flexibility to match the pacing to your story. Television news is constrained by time, so you often only have 75 to 90 seconds to tell your story. Sequences allow you to compress time and get to the detail of the story without changing the event. Sequences help maintain journalist credibility.

Editing in the camera also will help when you are producing your package. Think about the shot you are taking, the previous shot, and the next shot you need. Shoot for the edit. This will save time and be greatly appreciated if another person is editing your story.

Audio: A Sound Foundation

Photographers need to record sound as well as images. Most professional cameras allow you to capture at least two channels of audio. Digital video cameras often give the user several choices of audio quality. The higher the bit rate, the better the quality. Some camcorders offer four channels of audio, but the price you pay is that you get lower quality sound and a reduced bit rate. Audio is often more important than the video, so you should aim for the highest possible quality in your audio.

All of the video you shoot and use should include natural sound. The natural or wild sound is what you hear at a scene. It may only be the wind blowing or the leaves rustling, but it adds another dimension to the video. Remember, we want to convey a real experience to the viewer, and the sound is crucial to that experience.

To get the best sound, you need to use the correct microphone and have it in the best location. For newsgathering, you can use three basic types of microphones. No matter which one you choose, they are designed to be heard, not seen. The microphone should not enter the shot.

1 *Handheld or stick microphone.* This type of microphone is useful in conducting live spur-of-the-moment interviews. Most TV stations use the stick microphone as a billboard to promote the station. It is not the best approach for visual storytelling because it draws attention to itself. The viewer is drawn to follow the microphone as it moves on the screen.

2 *Lavaliere or clip-on microphone.* This type of microphone is less obtrusive than a stick microphone. These microphones offer the best way to hide the equipment and get it close to the source of the sound. The lavaliere is often used with a wireless transmitter. It can be clipped to your subjects to allow them the freedom to move around and do whatever they are doing. With a lavaliere microphone, your subjects will often forget they are wearing one and be more natural and not appear to act for the camera. Not only can you put a lavaliere on a person, but you can also use it to pick up audio from anything that makes a sound. For example, if you are doing a story about the tapping of trees to harvest the sap for maple syrup, a strategically placed microphone can get the sound of the sap falling into the bucket. Again, it brings viewers into the scene and lets them experience the story for themselves.

3 *The shotgun microphone.* The shotgun microphone is the most versatile microphone you can use. It is often mounted on the camera to pick up natural sound. But it can be used for gathering just about any type of sound in most situations. For interviews, the long pick-up pattern allows for good sound while keeping the microphone out of the picture. That also allows you to get sound from a scene without having to stop your subject to clip on a lavaliere. Some of the best sound you can get is with a shotgun microphone held just out of frame, but close enough to the source to hear it clearly.

120

No matter which microphone you choose, you usually need to get it close to the sound you want to record. Be aware of every sound at a scene. You want to be sure you are recording what you want. The noises the microphone picks up when you jostle it are distracting. The best way to know if your microphone is getting what you want is to use headphones while shooting. This is especially true when using a wireless system. Not only do you need to listen for interference or dying batteries, but you may also hear your subject saying something important to your story.

Mark Anderson, a network freelancer from Minneapolis, calls what he does "pinning the tail on the donkey." He finds a person at the scene of his story and asks him or her to wear the wireless microphone. While he is shooting, he listens for usable sound. When he hears a useful quote or bit of natural sound, he takes his microphone off and seeks out another person to pin it on. He is able to get some very compelling personalized sound by moving his microphone often and listening while he shoots.

Putting It All Together to Tell a Story

121

Four tools are essential for visual storytelling. In order of importance they are:

- The camera
- The microphone
- The edit suite
- The written word

When telling a story, use pictures as your first tool. Consider them the same way a novelist uses a pen or computer to capture the words for a book. What you can't tell with images, you tell through the sound using microphones. This sound can either be natural sounds gathered at the scene or interviews recorded in the field.

What cannot be told with the pictures and sound can be written while editing. The way they are put together during editing can help to tell the story. The last tool, in terms of visual storytelling, is the written word. You should use words to tell what cannot be seen or heard using the first three tools. NBC's Bob Dotson (2000) calls it "writing to the corners of your picture."

You should aim for steady, sequenced images with meaningful and compelling natural sound. Notice the word *steady*. It is important and separates professionally shot video from what amateurs take. Like the noises you get from handling a microphone, video shots that wobble and careen are distracting to your audience.

Video cameras that produce excellent quality images are available at department stores worldwide. It is how you use the camera that makes you a storyteller. The best way to keep an image steady is to use a tripod. A tripod also allows you to shoot longer. If you are tired and fatigued, you won't be able to shoot as well.

You can also use the world as your tripod. Dave Wertheimer, news director at KIMT-TV in Mason City, Iowa, looks for tripods everywhere while he is shooting. It might be the hood of a car, a parking meter, or a tree stump. Anything can be used to help keep your images stable.

Story Building

Every story needs a beginning, a middle, and an end. The best visual stories fulfill those needs with gripping images. You usually want to begin a story with an image that establishes the scene, character, and mood of the piece. The viewer should be intrigued enough to want to watch the whole story.

The middle is the meat of the story. It's where you introduce the characters, the conflict, and the resolution. Sequences are the foundation of the story in the middle of the story. The end is used to sum up the main idea of the story. Give the viewer a real sense of conclusion. Use the negative action of your subject walking away from the camera to show the end of the story. It may seem old fashioned, but the cowboy riding away into the sunset is an excellent way to end your story.

The most important part of your job as a photojournalist is to stay safe. You can't report if you are injured. Avoid situations that could put you in harm's way. Your life and limbs are not worth the price of getting an unusual angle or experiencing a hazardous confrontation. If covering a fire, keep a safe distance and use your tripod. Walls of buildings collapse and power lines fall when their supports burn away. Professional firefighters are trained to avoid these dangers. Pay attention to their direction while shooting.

Taping from helicopters and operating remote-broadcasting trucks also pose their own dangers. Insist that you be properly trained before operating such equipment.

Get to Work

While you are shooting, try to think about the whole story. Establish a thesis or commitment statement that conveys the idea of your story. Use a proper noun and a verb, and try to portray emotion. For a story about recycling you might have a commitment statement that reads, "Andy loves recycling aluminum cans." Try to stick to your commitment. Everything you shoot should support your commitment. Once you get started and are at a scene, your commitment may change. Realize the change and adapt to support the new commitment. Each time you go into the field, do your best to keep your audience in mind. Think of someone you know and then use your video, audio, and text to tell the story as if you were telling it to that person. By focusing on the audience you serve, you will find and tell far more interesting stories.

123

References

Dotson, B. (2000). *Make it memorable: Writing and packaging TV news with style.* Chicago: Bonus Books.

1 Shoot a scene in sequences, moving from the wide scene shot through the medium, close-up, and extreme close-up shots. Make sure you spend enough time with each shot to give yourself ample footage to choose from when you edit. Then, write a short paper to accompany your footage that explains what you've shot, how you've moved through the scene, and why you chose the pieces you did to tell the story.

2 Select an event that you think would be worth covering and then shoot it with your video camera. Find a variety of close-ups, scene setters, and other varied shots. When you are done shooting, review your video for strengths and weaknesses. What did you miss? What shots told the story best? Write a short paper that analyzes your findings. Also include ways in which you might have covered this event differently based on the medium for which you were shooting. For example, how would your approach differ if your images were to be Webcast, put on the nightly TV news, or used as stills for a newspaper or a Web site?

The Fort Wayne Freedom makes its grand entrance to the field in the Memorial Coliseum for its first playoff game on July 11, 2004. (Photograph courtesy of Will Vragovic.)

Editing for Moving Pictures

Legendary educational reformer John Dewey held a strong belief in "learning by doing." The students at the Chicago school he and his wife, Alice, ran learned as much chemistry, physics, and biology by cooking meals as they did in the laboratory setting. Dewey's ideas regarding the importance of practically based learning remain a valuable part of our learning system today.

Digital video editing requires an approach that mirrors the "learning by doing" process. Therefore, the majority of this chapter will have a "hands-on" feel as we give you a "walk-through" on how to engage in the process of digital video editing. While you can learn a great deal from this chapter, you will learn even more if you use it in connection with the Final Cut Pro editing system.

Before we begin learning about editing, however, we provide you with a brief review of the history of digital editing and some preparation you can undertake as you gather the material you plan to edit.

A Brief Look at Nonlinear Editing Software

For the first 10 years of desktop computer-based video editing, one brand name dominated the field: Avid. Loved, hated, or merely tolerated, the Avid systems could be found in the majority of professional video editing facilities. Media 100 and others had their admirers too, but Avid had the highest market share. Adobe's Premiere product was not considered a professional tool during this period.

The situation began to change at the spring 1999 National Association of Broadcasters conference when Apple Computer gave the curious a sneak peak at a new nonlinear editing (NLE) tool called Final Cut Pro (FCP). Unlike its would-be competitor, Apple did not rely on custom hardware to do its magic. The Final Cut Pro system was designed from the ground up to work with digital video. Avid's claim to fame was its ability to digitize an analog video source in real time at a high-quality level. This level was only limited by the amount of hard drive space an editor had available. The Apple system, by starting with a digital video (DV) source, only had to capture or transfer the digital video file from the DV source tape using a new type of connection called IEEE 1394 or FireWire. Perfect quality was preserved through this digital transfer. The DV tape was already compressed five to one at acquisition time in the camcorder, thus saving more file space than a high-quality analog-to-digital conversion. Avid would not have a competing product, at a similar price, for at least 9 months. The giant blinked and the rest, as they say, is history.

Apple's Final Cut Pro systems continue to have increasing popularity in "shops" of all sizes, from small operations to major network facilities. Final Cut Pro and its little brother, Final Cut Express, are used by tens of thousands of professional editors, teachers, and students every day. These editing programs help create the stories you will see on your TV tonight or on the big screen in the years to come. Due to this increasing acceptance and its outstanding ease of use, Final Cut Pro was chosen as the NLE application to be featured throughout the remainder of this chapter.

In the Field

Before the editing booth comes the shoot. While you can spend a great deal of time trimming that first edit, adding a fade to black or boosting the voiceover (VO) just a bit, if you don't bring good material into the booth, no technology in the world can save you.

Shooters should remember five simple things to make their editors' jobs a lot easier:

▶ Never record anything of importance in the first 10 seconds of any reel. Tapes stretch. When we all have hard disk–based ENG gear this will no longer be a problem, but until that glorious day, don't record anything of value in those first 10 seconds of tape.

▶ Each time you take a new shot, record *at least* 5 seconds of video prior to any actual on-camera action (i.e., an interview, a stand-up). Digital VCRs, just like their analog cousins, still take time to "get up to speed." Do not start a camera recording from Stop with the idea that you can "grab this great shot" just by hitting the red button. Also, leaving a video recorder in "Record/Pause" is a bad idea. The video head will needlessly have increased wear and the tape may develop some dreaded "dropouts" at the pause point. Plus, recording "an extra few seconds" prior to the action you really care about will give you some "pad" footage to use as a part of a video transition.

▶ Continue to "roll" for 5 seconds after the action is finished. This gives you some more pad footage for an exit transition.

4 Decide on the shotgun and external microphone channels and stick with these choices throughout a package. Better yet, use a general policy that states something like: "Shotgun on Channel 1, External Microphone on Channel 2."

▶ Know how to set your white balance manually and don't rely on an auto mode. Auto modes only adjust for average situations. Is your work average or do you want it to be a bit higher in quality? Also, white balance every time the lighting changes. This includes changes such as (a) indoor to outdoor, (b) daytime to nighttime, and (c) fluorescent to incandescent.

129

Part 1: The FCP Interface

Setup and Storage

The first step in the digital video editing process is to set up your system for video capture from your field tape. If you are working in a production facility or campus lab that has an engineering staff, this part of the process may already be completed for you. Otherwise, follow these three quick steps to ensure that your FCP system is ready for capture:

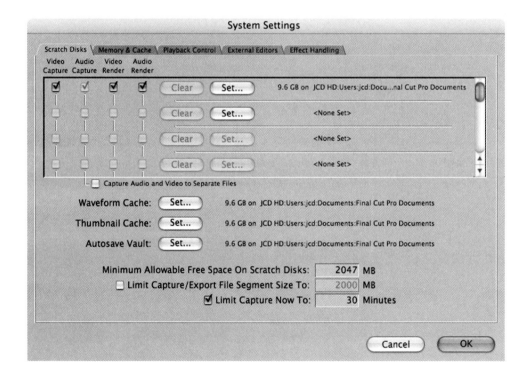

❶ Open the *Final Cut Pro HD Menu > System Settings...* dialog and check to see that the *Scratch Disks* settings have been set to their default locations. Often this location is a secondary internal hard drive or an external FireWire drive. It is good practice to create a folder with the name "Final Cut Pro

Documents" and then set or "point" all of your *Scratch Disk* items (Video Capture, Audio Capture, Video Render & Audio Render) to write to this folder.

2 Continue to set the remaining *Scratch Disk* items (Waveform Cache, Thumbnail Cache, and Autosave Vault) to point to the same "Final Cut Pro Documents" folder. The Autosave Vault setting is particularly important, because this is where FCP will place "autosaved" or backup copies of your current project. If you should have some kind of application or system crash, a copy of your project file can be found here.

3 Close the *System Settings* dialog and open the *Final Cut Pro HD Menu > Easy Setup . . .* dialog and confirm that "DV-NTSC" has been selected. Close the *Easy Setup* dialog.

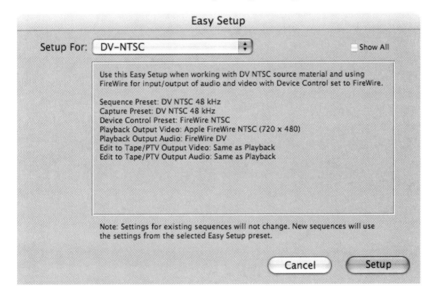

131

Capturing

Once system setup is complete, it is time to get ready to capture (i.e., transfer to your computer's hard drive) the digital video stream file that is recorded on your DV tape. Open the *File Menu > Log and Capture . . .* window and note the following items:

❶ *The VTR controls below the playback window.* The status display below the controls should read "VTR OK." If it reads "No Communication," your VTR is not on or not properly connected. Check to see that your VTR is properly powered up and that the FireWire cable is securely connected to both the VTR and your computer. Pushing Play ⓟ, or tapping the spacebar, engages the tape in the VTR. Pushing Stop ⓒ, or tapping the spacebar again, pauses the tape.

❷ Locate the Capture buttons in the lower right-hand corner.

❸ Three types of capturing are possible in Final Cut Pro: *Capture Now*, single *Clip* capture, and capture a *Batch* of Logged Clips. Each method has its advantages depending on the current situation. Playing a tape and clicking *Capture Now* causes the current audio and video to be immediately recorded on the *Scratch Disk*. To end the capture, just hit the Escape key in the upper left-hand corner of the keyboard. An "Untitled" file appears in the browser window. This file may then be single clicked and named.

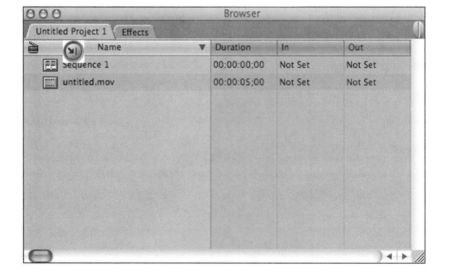

A *Capture Clip* differs from a *Capture Now* in that "IN" and "OUT" points must be set before a *Capture Clip* can occur. The advantages of *Capture Clip* over *Capture Now* are that (1) only the material you want is captured and (2) a file is named prior to capturing without the need for renaming. The *IN Point* controls are located in the lower left-hand portion of the Log and Capture window. Clicking the button (or tapping the *I* key on the keyboard) enters the *IN Point* of the current capture, while clicking on the INSERT button causes the VTR to go to the *IN Point*.

On the lower right-hand corner of the Log and Capture window are located the *OUT Point* controls. Clicking the button (or tapping the O key on the keyboard) enters the *OUT Point* of the current capture, while clicking on the button causes the VTR to go to the *OUT Point*. Once *IN* and *OUT* points have been set, clicking on *Capture Clip* will rewind the VTR (if necessary) and record audio and video from the *IN Point* to the *OUT Point* onto the *Scratch Disk*. To end the capture prior to the *OUT Point*, just hit the *Escape* key in the upper left-hand corner of the keyboard.

A *Capture Batch* differs from *Capture Clip* in that several *IN* and *OUT* points may be set prior to capturing through a process called *logging*. Logging clips in advance of capturing is a wonderful way to access your field footage as a whole. By capturing a series of clips, *Capture Batch* encourages the capture of only "good" clips, keeping the *Scratch Disk* space to a minimum. Also, by logging a series of clips prior to a batch capture, the capture process itself may proceed unattended, while you are free to focus on another activity.

IN and *OUT* points during a *Capture Batch* are set the same way as for a *Capture Clip* except that the *Log Clip* button is pressed after each new set of points is entered. Pressing *Log Clip* pauses the tape playback, and causes a new *Offline Clip* to be added to the *Browser*. It is good practice to name your clips ending with a number (e.g., "Scene01"). FCP will automatically increment your clip name with a new sequential number as new clips are added.

133

Capturing your field footage to the *Scratch Disk* is one of the first, if not one of the most important, steps in the NLE digital video editing process. The next step is where the editing itself truly begins: moving clips into a sequence.

The Timeline

Select *File > New > Sequence* to create a new sequence. Note the following critical areas of the timeline:

1 *The Name Tab.* This tab, located in the upper left-hand corner of the sequence, shows the name of the sequence, the current playback head position (here at "01:00:01;14" indicating the

134

playback head is 1 second and 14 frames from the start of the sequence), and the "Render Quality Button,"  which is discussed later.

2 The *Timeline* has at least one video and two audio layers present. Video clips are added to the timeline to create sequences.

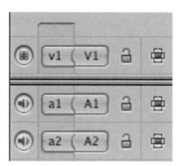

Clips, once captured or imported may be dragged directly from the browser into a sequence. Clip placement within a sequence is determined by two parameters: location of the "playback head" and the designated destination layers. If you have only one video layer and two audio layers, by default these will be your destination layers. Otherwise, check to see that the *Source Control Buttons* are matched to the appropriate video and audio layers.

Simply drag an audio  or video  source selector to the appropriate audio or video layer.

3 The *Linking* [icon] and *Snapping* [icon] buttons/indicators are located in the opposite upper right-hand corner of the Sequence Window.

If a clip is dragged into a layer with "snapping on" (toggle the N key) , the clip will seem to "snap" into place at the edge of a clip currently in the layer. With linking on (toggle the L key), a video clip and any associated audio clips are treated in the timeline as a set, allowing audio and video to remain in "sync." Dragging clips one at a time from the browser into a sequence is fine for simple insert editing, but if a more sophisticated technique is desired, the "drag to the Canvas Window," discussed next, is the preferred method.

The Canvas Window

Normally the *Canvas Window* is the area of the FCP interface where sequence playback occurs. Wherever the playback head is positioned, that frame of the sequence is shown in the *Canvas Window*. The window also serves as a "drop zone" for clips that are being dragged from the browser. This "drag-and-drop" technique allows one of five different types of edits to occur depending on which exact "drop area" the video clip is released in.

135

An *Insert Edit* command literally inserts the dragged clip at the playback head position of the target track. Inserting will cause any video (and linked audio) to be split at the insertion point, pushing any current clips in the sequence to the right to "make room" for the incoming clips(s). Dragging to the *Overwrite Edit* area will cause the incoming clip to be placed at the playback head location overwriting any current clip(s) to the right. Multiple clip(s) will be overwritten to exactly match the length of the incoming clip.

Dropping a dragged clip on the *Replace Edit* area will cause the overwrite of only the current clip in a sequence up to the length of this current clip. Note that, during a *Replace Edit*, the incoming clip must be as least as long as the current clip. If an incoming clip is shorter, an error message will appear stating "Insufficient content for edit." A *Fit to Fill Edit* is much like a *Replace Edit*, except that *the duration* of the incoming clip will be adjusted to match that of the current clip.

Incoming clips for *Fit to Fill Edits* will therefore be speeded up or slowed down to match the length of the current clip.

The final Canvas Window "drag-and-drop" technique, the *Superimpose Edit*, places an incoming clip in the layer immediately above the current target layer. The incoming clip for a *Superimpose Edit* must be at least as long as the distance from the playback head location in the timeline to the end of the last clip in the upper layer. If an incoming clip is shorter than this distance, an error message will appear stating "Insufficient content for edit." Any transparent areas of an incoming clip placed with a *Superimpose Edit* command will "composite" with clips on lower layers (e.g., Photoshop still graphics or video clips with alpha channels—see the discussion later in this chapter on filters and transitions for more details).

On the bottom edge of the *Canvas Window* are the *Timeline VTR Controls.* Left to right, the controls are *Go to the IN Point* of the sequence , *Play IN to OUT* , *Play* , *Play Around Current Frame* , and *Go to the OUT Point* . (Note that the *Go to the IN Point* and the *Go to the OUT Point* arrows point in the opposite direction here from those found in the *Capture Window*. This is because here we are interested in the IN and OUT points of an entire sequence, instead of a single clip.

On either side of the *Canvas Window* VTR Controls are the sequence *Jog* and *Shuttle* *Controls*. The *Jog Control* may be "scrubbed" side to side with the mouse allowing you to view the sequence at the playback head position one frame at a time. The *Shuttle Control* allows the playback head to move at very high speed to quickly navigate an entire sequence in the timeline.

137

The Viewer Window

Anytime during the editing process, individual clips may be viewed in the *Viewer Window*, normally located to the immediate left of the *Canvas Window*. When a clip located in the *Browser* or *Timeline Windows* is double-clicked, it is immediately available for viewing. Viewed clips that are already on the *Timeline*, and thus part of a sequence, will have an indicator like this: in the *Viewer Timeline Area* along the bottom edge of *Viewer*. VTR controls, similar to those found on the *Canvas Window* are located here as well. The *Viewer Window* also has other functions; for instance, this is the area where controls for audio, filters, transitions, and simple motion are found on a series of tabs.

The Toolbar
Once clips have been placed in a sequence, they may be manipulated using any of these most commonly used tools found in *The Toolbar:*

Arrow (Selection) Tool

Track Select Tool

Razor Blade Tool

Zoom Tool

138

The *Arrow Tool* selects a single clip in a sequence. The *Track Select Tool* selects an entire track forward, reverse, both directions, or multiple tracks forward through repeated taps on the *T* key. The *Razor Blade Tool* divides single or multiple clips in half. The *Zoom Tool* magnifies or shrinks the entire timeline view.

Part 2: The NLE Process

Now that you have been introduced to the basic elements of the FCP interface, I would like to guide you through a sample news story edit session using Final Cut Pro. Once your video is shot, captured, and placed in a project, the real fun begins: the editing process itself. Typically, you or your videographer will have shot an interview or two, some "B" roll (video images shot to accompany reporter or anchor script), perhaps a public speech, or simply a "stand-up" with you talking directly to the camera. These elements can be quickly combined in FCP to produce an exciting, informative "package" (assuming that your source material is exciting and informative).

Your Assignment: A Night House Fire in a New Upscale Neighborhood
From the first moment you arrive on the scene things look chaotic. Live units from several other local TV news organizations are already there. Flames have engulfed the still striking, three-story home. Your first

job is to get some "B" roll because the fire department is already busy putting the fire out. Be careful. Don't get too close. Make sure that you get enough "B" roll (20 minutes or more) to include with any voiceovers from interviews that you will be shooting soon. Make sure the camera is on manual iris and check the video levels in the viewfinder. The flames will be quite bright against the night sky, so let them almost go completely white. Stay with a wide-angle view to emphasize how immense the fire is—this is your cover shot. Be ready to zoom in should a particular part of the structure look like it is starting to collapse. Once you have shot the fire itself, it is time to find potential interviewees. If you are lucky enough to have a videographer, you should start looking for people to talk to as soon as you arrive while the videographer shoots the fire itself.

The fire chief is very busy at this point so don't bother him or any of the other firefighters. Start looking around for any other officials you might see. Police officers are usually a good choice at a fire scene because once they've secured the scene, they need to wait until the fire is out to begin the next stage of their work. You find an officer just next to where you have parked. Grab your videographer and bring him or her over to set up for a few questions.

139

The officer tells you that no one was living here yet and that the police department has no clues at this point. However, he does tell you that a small car was reported driving in the area just a few minutes prior to the fire being spotted. A neighbor now walks up, recognizes you "from the TV" and makes a motion that he has something to tell you. Fred, the owner of the house just across the street from the burning building, says, "I saw someone running across my front yard just before I heard a car starting down the block." One of the firefighters now passes by your position and is heard to say, "It was all over the place, like someone had sprayed it in every room." You keep the camera rolling as another neighbor walks up.

Shirley, who lives three doors down the street, says that she did not see or hear anything prior to the fire trucks arriving. However, her 13-year-old son was shooting some late-night hoops when he ran out in the street to pick up the ball. He had not heard the car approaching and the driver had to swerve to miss him. He had already told a police officer what he saw.

The fire has now been brought under control and will be out in another half-hour. A few firefighters remain on the scene to "overspray the structure" for the next few hours until daylight. You make a note to tell the assignment desk to send back another videographer in the morning to get some aftermath shots while the fire crew is still on the scene. The fire chief has now signaled that he is willing to take a few questions. Tim from Channel 18, your biggest competitor, asks the obvious question: "Chief, do we know how the fire started?" The chief responds: "I would prefer to let the arson investigators do their job first before we begin speculating."

"But, Chief," you ask, "something was found sprayed in every room, wasn't it?" "How did you know that?" the Chief snapped. "Oh, well, and this is strictly off the record" (you raise your hand to cover the still rolling camera lens) "we did find something rather odd. Someone seems to have spray painted the same words in every room of the house." "What did it say, Chief?" you ask. "I've said enough already." He quickly turns to walk off and rejoin the other firefighters.

Early the next morning, you call in to the assignment desk and ask if a video crew has gone back to the site of last night's big house fire. The desk manager confirms that a live unit is currently on the scene. You quickly get dressed and drive over. You have an idea. You grab the videographer, Cheryl, and have her change cameras. Cheryl, the senior photographer at the station, also does a bit of freelance work on the side. She always carries her own camcorder with an extra long telephoto lens to use when she shoots the occasional kayak race on weekends.

You have Cheryl pop a tape in the camera and then you walk with her around to the rear of the now blackened house. You tell her to zoom in as tight as she can through a big window on the home's lower level. The sun is behind you this early in the day. Cheryl lowers the camera to steady the shot on a tripod setup just outside the police line. "What are we looking for?" she asks. "I'll know it when I see it," you proclaim. Suddenly Cheryl takes a deep breath and says, "I think I see something." She then mutters to herself, "That makes no sense," but she records what she sees. Once she has a few good takes, she motions you to the viewfinder. You see exactly what you were looking for. You ask for her tape and run back to your car. Back at the station you hurry in to find an open edit suite and sit down with all of your tapes. While Final Cut Pro is launching, you remember that there is going to be an emergency press conference about the fire at 10 a.m. Because you normally do not work the day shift, another reporter will be covering the conference. You call the assignment desk and ask them who is going. It's Barbara, the noon anchorwoman who also happens to be good friends with Bill, the local police spokesperson. You grab a two-way radio at the assignment desk and call for Barb. When she answers, you tell her to ask Bill one simple question: "Have you found the car?" Bill answers, "Yes," so you tell Barb to ask him, "Was it one of those new hybrids?" "Yes," Bill answers. "How did you know that, Barb?" She answers, "Just a lucky guess," with a big smile on her face.

Final Cut Pro is now running and you begin to *Log and Capture* your tapes. You are careful to name your first clip with a trailing number so that FCP will automatically increment the remaining captures. You really want to start editing, but you decide to run a batch capture so that all of your footage is in the computer. You take the time to make a preliminary shot list while the clips are recorded to your scratch drive. The cover shot of the fire when you first arrived will be followed by the on-site witnesses and then the brief comment from the police officer. Your "stand-up" at the fire scene this morning comes next.

The captures are completed and you begin to drag your clips to the timeline. As you assemble your clips you double-click on each one, sending them to the *Viewer Window*. You tap the Audio tab to check sound levels. Everyone sounds good except for the interview with Shirley, so you decide to raise her 3 dB using the *Level Control* option at the top of the *Viewer Window*.

Now comes the big shot that may just boost your career and help the police as well. You reach for the final tape that was shot just this morning and load it into the VCR. This time, you hit *Capture Now* as soon as the image of the back on the house pops up in the *Log and Capture Window*. There is it, the faint image you were waiting for. You hit the *Escape* key to stop the capture. Next, you single click the new Untitled clip in the *Browser* and name it. It's showtime.

Dragging the new clip, Fire_27, to the *Canvas Window*, you make an *Insert Edit* just prior to your standup footage. With Fire_27 now the timeline, you double-click to send it to the *Viewer Window*.

You go to the *Browser* again and select the *Effects* tab. Scrolling down to the *Video Filters/Perspective* folder, you find what you have been looking for, the *Mirror* effect.

141

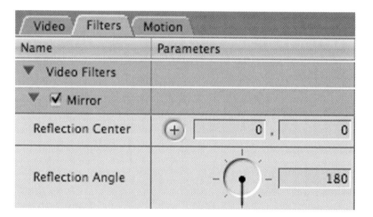

You drag this effect to the *Viewer Window* and click on the *Filters* tab.

You turn the rotation angle control to read 180°. Now you look at the Canvas Window to see the result. Sure enough, it worked! Although the image is still faint and will need to have its brightness raised (using the Brightness and Contrast filter in the *Video Filters/Image Control* folder), you can now read the words outlined on the surface of the dining room mirror: "Less is best," the calling card of an eco-terrorist group that had previously threatened to make trouble for this construction project. You quickly trim the remaining clips and select *Print to Video* in the *File Menu* to record your masterpiece back to tape.

Conclusion

Final Cut Pro is a very powerful tool, but it is only as powerful as the stories that you have to tell. The software itself can't save you, but the more time you spend with it, the easier certain tasks will become. In "learning by doing" you will have the opportunity to expand your skill set and tell your good stories in the best way possible.

For Further Reading

Brenneis, L. (2004). *Final Cut Pro HD for Mac OS X: Visual QuickPro guide.* Berkeley, CA: Peachpit Press.

Weynand, D. (2004). *Apple Pro training series: Final Cut Pro HD.* Berkeley, CA: Peachpit Press.

143

1 Take the video you shot for Exercise 1 in Chapter 8 and edit it twice. First, edit a scene that is as short as possible but still tells the story well. Then, reedit your video to be as long as possible without being tedious. For example, if there is an action shot that takes 10 seconds, you could edit it to be composed of two 5-second shots or you could use many shots to examine the action from a variety of angles, which might take almost 20 seconds. Work with your video to see what you can come up with.

2 At this stage in the book, you have been exposed to all three components of crafting a broadcast news package (broadcast writing, video shooting, and video editing). Find an event you think is newsworthy and craft a complete package that would be ready for broadcast. Remember, packages last about a minute and a half, so you'll need both words and video that can cover that amount of time. It's a lot harder than it looks. Shoot your video, craft your script, and then put it all together. After you are done, write a short paper that analyzes what you did. What worked well and what could have used a little help? Spend some time examining what you would like to improve on when you create your next package.

Students gather at Shafer Tower on Ball State campus to honor the life of Karl Harford on March 9, 2004. Harford was a Ball State student shot by him three people to whom he gave a ride home from a party. The men robbed of $2 before killing him. About 200 people attended the ceremony, including Harford's parents. (Photograph courtesy of Will Vragovic.)

Multimedia Journalism: Putting It All Together

A combination of sound, image, text, and interactivity—hereafter referred to as multimedia journalism—gives media practitioners a new way to tell stories, using the strengths of each medium to produce a more compelling package. From the outset, a multimedia journalist must appreciate the potential and power of each medium and capitalize on those strengths. In doing so the multimedia reporter produces journalism that is well beyond what a single medium can do. The multimedia reporter needs to know how to use a variety of digital tools, but the essential requirement is a multimedia mind-set. Loosely articulated, this mind-set requires the ability to conceive of stories that go beyond a single medium when it is appropriate to use more than one medium. Sometimes one medium is sufficient to provide what audiences need. Implicit in this statement is an understanding of audiences (note the plural form) and an acceptance that the fundamental role of journalism remains constant, which is to inform, educate, and entertain.

The multimedia form of reporting was relatively rare as of mid-2005. Similarly, the kind of reporter who is comfortable and proficient in all media tends to be rare. The good ones attract better salaries and attention from their editors. We can safely say that as convergence develops, media organizations will welcome people who appreciate the power of each medium and who are willing to embrace a multimedia form of reporting. Multimedia journalism will evolve into a richer form of journalism as the century evolves.

Chapter 2 detailed the strengths and weaknesses of each medium. When telling multimedia stories, it is vital to appreciate and use each medium's strengths. To recap: Print is portable and permanent. It offers depth and detail but it is limited in the sense that the news is only as recent as the last print run. It also requires effort on the part of the audience to absorb the information. Television and radio are immediate and emotional. They take you to the scene and provide images and sound, but they are also ephemeral. They disappear into the ether once you see or hear the events they describe, and the entertainment element of broadcast can be distracting. Online combines the immediacy of broadcast with print's capacity to give people detail and background. Plus, it can be interactive if journalists know how to use this power appropriately and well. In many cases, this remains a big *if.* Interactivity could be the key to producing successful multiple-platform stories. It gives journalists the chance to relate to, and link with, audiences. It requires television audiences to do more than the passive act of watching. Audiences could be asked to add perspective to the story or to interact with the story and become involved via a quiz or interactive graphic.

Journalists need to educate themselves to think in terms of multimedia reporting. This is one of the changes of mind-set mentioned earlier in this chapter. You need to approach every story looking for potential multimedia coverage. This may involve moving beyond the classic narrative structure. All traditional forms of journalism, be they the text, still photographs, and graphics of newspaper and magazine reporting; or the video, audio, animated graphics, and words of television, tell stories in a linear form. The storytelling follows a classic narrative pattern: a beginning, middle, and end. Both also deliver information one way. The audience has few ways to provide feedback beyond the traditional format of letters to the editor or station. Both are tethered to production structures that compel audiences to organize their lives around the product rather than when it suits them. People must watch television news at a time that suits the broadcaster, although cable television attempts to deal with that by offering a cycle of news. Magazines and newspapers have expended huge amounts of energy in the past few decades to make their products look attractive—witness the revolution in newspaper and magazine design in the past generation. That beauty, however, only becomes apparent when someone makes the effort to read the newspaper or magazine. Magazines often end up as landfill or as decorations in dentists' waiting rooms, while newspapers have an even shorter shelf life, destined to end up at the bottom of a birdcage. Television news disappears into oblivion unless we remember to record the program.

Multimedia journalism represents a different form of storytelling and a different form of narrative structure. It also is available, when archived online, for rediscovery and redistribution. Because of its non-linear format, it welcomes interactivity and two-way communication. Audiences can play with it, play it over and over again, and add their feedback and comments. Best of all, it responds to many more of the senses. We can hear, we can see, and because of the emotional impact of good video, we can also feel.

How does one become a multimedia journalist? The key is the willingness to think in terms of the strengths and power of each medium. It requires learning new skills and, therefore, training becomes vital. You may have to teach yourself or seek help from colleagues, because traditionally employers have not offered much training to journalists. Martha Stone, training director for the Newsplex at the University of South Carolina, believes that much multimedia journalism is bubbling up from the grassroots of news organizations on an experimental basis, not as a planned, long-term investment in the future. "Few multimedia journalists are being trained on video cameras, audio recorders, and cross-platform writing styles," she noted. "To improve multimedia journalism," Stone said, "a commitment from the top levels of management is needed" (2002).

149

If your employer or university offers training, grab every opportunity. Remember that as a human being, as well as a journalist, if you are not expanding you are contracting. If employers or universities do not offer training in the latest tools, then get together with like-minded colleagues. If you are interested in a particular software package or digital camera, for example, organize a brown-bag lunch session. Scour the Web for tips. Attend one of the many seminars and workshops offered by places like the Poynter Institute, the American Press Institute, or similar organizations. Web sites are listed at the end of the chapter.

After you absorb the skills, what happens next? As Chapter 2 explains, news in a converged newsroom is event driven, so the significance of the news will determine the extent and nature of the coverage. The key people are the editors who assign the individuals or teams to cover each event. This means that these assignment editors must have a multimedia mind-set and must also be aware of the strengths and limitations of each medium. As multimedia journalist and educator Jane Stevens noted, these people must know "what's possible, what's impossible, and how to integrate that into a minute-by-minute, hourly, daily, weekly, and long-term flow of news, information and storytelling." Stevens believes newsrooms will have many options for covering stories, but she suggests two basic models: producer-driven stories and reporter-driven stories (2002). Note the tendency in a converged operation to borrow terminology from both broadcast and print. That is simply the nature of the new medium—it cherry-picks ideas. Producer-driven stories work best for breaking news and daily news content. For example, when the hurricanes and storms hit Florida in 2004, the producer or assignment editor would dispatch a team of reporters to cover the story. "Each takes a small digital video camera, but the best videographers are sent to the heart of the action, so are the best [and] most experienced writers," Stevens said. Less experienced reporters, all equipped with video cameras, would be sent to outlying areas. All of the reporters would file text, video clips, audio clips, and still photos. The producer would assemble them into a package, along with material provided by graphic artists and interactive computer specialists. "Short text stories and some video clips may go out on the Web immediately after they are filed," Stevens said. "Comprehensive reports tallying dead and injured and detailing economic effects are filed later."

The reporters would file what they found. On many occasions, they would be unaware of how much of their contribution was published or in what form. The producer back at headquarters would be like a great chef, creating a masterpiece by using items from many parts of the country. This was certainly the case during the war in Iraq, where journalists were told to transmit in short bursts, according to poynter.org. While the reporters sent back bits and pieces when they could, producers in the United States assembled packages from a host of sources in various parts of the world.

A reporter-driven story involves a single reporter or small team. The team assembles a package that it controls from start to finish. Stevens (2002) notes that sometimes reporters work from the scene of the event if the scenario is sufficiently compact that a handful of reporters can cover it. Sometimes the story is assembled at the office, where people have worked on an investigation or major project over many months. Sometimes the situation involves an individual working in an isolated region or embedded with troops during a war. "It may be an international reporter who works alone, or it may be a team of reporters comprising videographers, computer graphics specialists and top writers who work on a series that's designed for different platforms from the start," Stevens explained. "The series may be delivered as one-minute videos on a news roundup that teases to a longer multimedia package." The format may vary, but the process remains the same: The reporter is given significant individual responsibility. Reporters use multimedia tools to produce a new form of journalism, but it is still journalism. It is necessary here to note the increasing importance of teams. In some situations a story becomes so big it requires a team of journalists. Part of the multimedia mind-set is the willingness to work with others and to share resources and knowledge.

BBC Television introduced a variation of Stevens's second concept at the start of the new century via their Video Journalist (VJ) program. This consists of a single person in the field who reports, shoots, writes, edits, and transmits stories. The program, known as PDP or Personal Digital Production, began in September 2001. The BBC established a training center at Newcastle in the north of England and planned to train about 600 of its more than 2,400 television journalists by early 2005. The VJ concept was the brainchild of Michael Rosenblum, a former NBC producer turned consultant. He convinced the BBC that it could boost newsgathering efficiency by using VJs. The idea was not to replace teams of traditional television crews, but to supplement them with mobile individuals. Rosenblum said the scheme was an attempt to "build television along the lines of a newspaper" operation. "We want to take them [reporters] out of the newsroom and put them in the field where they can gather news," he said. Rosenblum told *Broadcast Engineering* magazine that his idea would cut the cost of production by 20 to 70 percent (2004).

Paul Myles (2004), the PDP center coordinator based at the BBC's Newcastle office, said video journalists mostly used Avid DV Express 3.5.4 nonlinear editing software, though some offices operated Macintosh-based systems and edited with Apple Computer's Final Cut Pro. Each course in the VJ program lasted 3 weeks. During the course, VJs were supplied with a digital video camera. Initially, they received the Sony PD150, but starting in 2004, attendees received a later model, the PD170. "It's a lightweight camera that records in DVCAM and

151

has two channels of audio," Myles said of the PD170, "We make several alterations to the basic camera. We have replaced the onboard Sony domestic microphone with a Seinhesser 416 microphone. It's a sensitive and directional microphone that helps us acquire excellent actuality." Myles's team also added a wide-angle lens and lens hood. "This allows us to get closer to the subjects we are filming, providing the benefits of a steadier shot, better depth of field, clearer audio and greater intimacy with character," he said.

Myles said VJs mainly contributed to the BBC's 6:30 p.m. regional news programs rather than the main late evening programs, but they also filed to current affairs, political, Welsh language, and children's programs. "The range of stories and techniques are almost as numerous as the trainees themselves," he said. "Many find the access and the ability to tell stories through real people's eyes the big attraction. For the others, multiple deployments are a big draw offering the ability to show several dimensions of a story simultaneously." Myles said the flexibility offered by the nonlinear editing systems helped producers create "very individual styles." He emphasized that video journalists were not intended to replace television news crews, but to supplement traditional ways of working and to offer more "up-close-and-personal" stories. "It is inevitable that the use of 'self-operating' staff will reduce the use of traditional crews but this wasn't the reason for doing it. The big attraction was that this way of working would give greater access, more freedom and creativity to the video-journalist, and a more honest and interesting final product," Myles said (2004).

Does this move by one of the world's biggest news organizations mean that the backpack journalist will become the norm? Probably not, but this form of journalism is becoming more common. Various media commentators have discussed how the scenario might evolve. Howard Tyner, who recently retired as vice president for editorial at the giant Tribune Co., said the notion of all journalists becoming one-man bands was ridiculous, because it was not possible for one person to produce top-quality content across all the media platforms. "Anyone who's ever gone out to cover a spot story thinking they could take pictures as well as notes knows how that's almost impossible," he said. He acknowledged that as journalism schools increasingly prepared their students for multimedia newsrooms, media companies would hire people with skills in more than one discipline. "We found that there were a number of people in [the Tribune Company] newsrooms who were hired to write stories, but had the ability and interest to deliver an astonishingly professional TV news spot," he said. "Not many of them, but they're there and more will be coming. I think if I were coming into journalism now I would supplement whatever my basic interest might be—newspaper reporting, broadcast reporting—with as much as I could learn about how to produce web-based news reports." Tyner expected that in the next few years reporters would cover stories for their newspaper or TV station but be asked to create actual Web reports with video and audio in addition to doing a more traditional report (Tyner 2004).

Gil Thelen, publisher of the *Tampa Tribune*, believes multimedia skills are more likely to be needed in newsrooms in smaller markets. "As you go up the size scale of media organizations, the skills tend to become narrower," he said. The main skill Thelen said he was looking for when hiring was craft mastery—being proficient in one aspect of journalism. It was vital, he said, for journalism schools to prepare graduates capable of doing craft-level work, but students also needed to have what he called a multimedia literacy. "Not mastery, but an awareness of how the various media work" he said. "Broadcast journalists need to be able to write a fundamental print story. Print people need to be able to be able to do a simple stand-up. I call that multimedia literacy." Students also needed to be lifelong learners and to be comfortable working in teams, Thelen said (2004).

Nora Paul, who directs the new media program at the University of Minnesota, believes the multi-skilled journalist is not a new idea. "It's the old one-man band at television stations," she said, where some people were expected to be able to shoot and report. Paul said people needed to get away from thinking in terms of the medium in which journalists delivered their product, "and then how can that be delivered best to a variety of platforms." Paul said it was silly for reporters to identify themselves as a broadcast journalist or a print journalist. "That's a ridiculous thing in this world where broadcast journalists are going to end up online, and print journalists' work is going to be part of the web site," she said. The more relevant distinction was whether someone was a word or a visual person. "If you are the visual person then you need a clear understanding of how best a visual works in print, [and] how it translates for online and then what plays well for TV, just as the word person needs to know what kind of lead works best for a newspaper versus online versus if you're writing for television." Paul said this was a more feasible way to think about multimedia "and all journalists need to know how the other media works to combine and serve the story in whatever platform. I think the biggest challenge is moving print people from production-line thinking to collaborative thinking in terms of creating news stories" (2004).

Professor Bob Papper of Ball State University has long been an advocate for convergence. He created and teaches some of the first convergent journalism courses in the country. He believes the multi-skilled journalist has a future, but he's just not sure how many will be needed. Papper noted that from a business standpoint, multimedia reporters were attractive because they could do many jobs. "From a realistic standpoint the more skills a person has, the less likely they are to be able to produce quality in all or any one area," he said. "The more skills a journalist has to use, the less time they can put into any one of those things." Papper said a role exists for a person who can do everything. These individuals might find more opportunities in smaller markets, where resources are scarce. "If you're hiring a bunch of people, you're probably going to get more quality and efficiency out of specialization, especially in a large market. In small markets this kind of journalism may work" (2004).

154

Martha Stone (2002), training director for the Newsplex, believes the model of the "do-it-all" journalist offers too many problems. "While some multimedia journalists can handle a variety of tasks efficiently and professionally, most will only deliver mediocre journalism," she said. "While some may excel at writing the story for print or broadcast, they may produce poor-quality video or still pictures." Stone believes that specialization, where people concentrated on one form of reporting, has stood the test of time: "Quality comes from those journalists who practice a defined job, be it writer, videographer, photographer or editor," she said. Kerry Northrup, who helped establish the Newsplex at the University of South Carolina, noted that the multimedia role tended to be the most controversial at newspapers. "For the average journalist it means more work and they won't pay me any extra," he said. However, an increasing number of journalists were adopting this model, he said, and these people sometimes demanded premium salaries. "It is unfeasible to expect that everyone will do this," he said. "People have strengths. There will be multi-faceted journalists, but a lot of people will be specialists." But all journalists needed to understand the relative strengths and weaknesses of the various media, and the various technologies that permitted newsgathering and distribution over all four points of what he called the convergence compass—print, video, online, and mobile. "You have to be multiple-media minded," he said. "The best writer in the world who refuses to have or share ideas for how to tell stories in other media is not as useful as someone with a multiple mind-set" (2004).

Northrup emphasizes that multimedia storytelling involves new workflows as well as learning new skills. This requires better use of resources and reorganizing newsrooms to turn them into information-based operations. He warned that journalists and editorial managers needed to "preserve their ethics while adapting to the increasingly numbing pace of media change and innovation." Northrup has created four job descriptions for convergent journalism: *newsflow manager, storybuilder, newsresourcer,* and *multi-skilled reporter.* He intentionally created new terms because with existing words "people tend to think the old way," while new words produced new ideas (2004).

The fourth job description applies to this chapter, so we will skim over the first three before discussing the fourth in detail. We need the first three to place the fourth in context. The newsflow manager is like television's executive producer with the added perspective of helicopter vision to oversee all stories in all media. This ensures that individual stories receive whatever resources they need. This manager chooses the most appropriate way to cover a story. The storybuilder is like a television field producer or newspaper editor who supervises individual stories (often more than one at a time), coordinating the various staff for each specific story. The newsresourcer is a data specialist who collects and distributes information from archives, databases, the Internet, and other sources for all journalists and editors in a newsroom. In summary, the newsflow manager concentrates on the overview of the story, the storybuilder focuses on the experience of the story, the newsresourcer provides the context for the story, and the multimedia journalist provides the content.

The multi-skilled reporter understands the strengths and weaknesses of each medium. He or she is skilled at interviewing and collecting still images, video, and audio. This reporter can edit those sounds and images, and can write stories to be distributed across multiple forms of media. With breaking news, the first reporter at the site needs to be able to capture as much information as possible in as many media forms as possible and then be able to deliver the story immediately. Convergence researcher Augie Grant noted that freelancers have always had this combination of skills and carried them "onto the battlefield and into remote regions, sometimes being a sole witness to a story that can and should be delivered across media." The multi-skilled reporter

155

needs the ability to tell any story in any form, including the inverted pyramid for newspapers, a standard broadcast narrative, and a Web version. "Writing across media may be one of the most difficult skills to master, but the task is made easier by the presence of story builders, editors, and others who can help refine the story for presentation," Grant said (2004).

When news breaks, journalists need to know which medium to feed first. Communication with managers is vital, aided considerably by satellite and cell phones. CNN reporters typically deliver a live television report, record a follow-up report, rewrite their script for the Web, and then feed for a radio network, all in the space of an hour or two, Grant said (2004). It is unlikely that all journalists would be expected to master all the skills related to gathering information. "Indeed, many news directors [and] editors say they do not expect every journalist to do everything," Grant said. In converged newsrooms, it is more likely that journalists will need a set of skills for handling basic stories. They also need to know when to call for help if the story develops beyond their basic skills. In collaboration with their newsflow manager, they would decide on the necessary backup to deal with the situation, much like the first police officer at a crime scene. Multi-skilled journalists need to know how to operate basic newsgathering tools. To that end, each year the Newsplex assembles the Ifra NewsGear. For more information, see the Newsplex details in the Web references at the end of the chapter.

Multimedia Skills

The most fundamental skill a multimedia reporter needs, as Chapter 3 explained, is the ability to write. If you can write well for one platform, you can write well for any platform. What about technical skills? In some respects, the technology is becoming relatively simple, and it is more important to know how to conceive ideas than it is to use the tools. If we must talk about the tools, the multimedia journalist needs to be able to take still and moving images. This will involve various forms of digital cameras. Allied with the digital still camera is the need to know how to use Photoshop. Possessing strong Photoshop skills will enable you to rescue poor images and to enhance good images. Some photographs will appear on the Web, others in print and as stills for television. Photoshop should be one of the first software packages that the aspiring multimedia journalist learns. Much Web production is template driven, with journalists inserting content into preordained holes, so this chapter will not advocate for any specific Web authoring tools, apart from recommending Dreamweaver as an easy-to-use and intuitive product.

Diffusion of innovation theory shows that people adopt products that are easy to use. To that end, this book recommends Final Cut Pro as the digital video editing tool for Macintosh-based journalists. Sadly it is not yet available for the PC. A range of audio editing tools is available. Again, we will avoid recommending any specific software apart from suggesting that the simplest to use is often the most satisfying.

When editing image and sound files, storage becomes a key issue. Despite the improved speed of FireWire cables for transferring files from camera to laptop, technology that involves drag and drop may be faster. So investigate hard drive–based technology that allows you to transfer files straight from the hard drive of the camera (video or still) to your laptop or desk computer. NewsGear offers some useful recommendations.

The Multimedia Process

Key to the whole concept of the multi-skilled journalist remains the mind-set that the information being gathered will be distributed via a variety of media, combined with recognition of the individual elements that must be captured to bring the story to the audience. The ability to look at a story or news event to determine what needs to be gathered and distributed for each medium is the final piece of the puzzle for the convergent journalist. This part of the chapter looks at this process and recommends an approach.

The first thing to remember is the primacy of information. In the multimedia world, the reporter cannot have too much information. You need as much information as possible because you do not know how many versions of the story you may be covering, and different media require different forms of information. Before you leave the office, work with your newsresourcer or newspaper library researcher to ask them to find as much information as they can about your story while you are in the field and ask them to contact you once they've found it. Cell phones and text messaging are helpful in this process. At the scene, gather everything you can find: documents, photographs, brochures, and Web addresses. Everything may prove useful, so adopt a pack-rat mentality. It's always easier to get details at the scene rather than when you return to the newsroom. Get as much of this information in digital form as possible. Always ask for digital files, and carry a thumb-sized storage device on your key chain for those occasions when officials offer you access to their computers. As of early 2005 most suppliers were selling 1-gigabyte key-chain storage devices. Accept paper documents as a last resort.

Carry a small digital voice recorder or mini-disc at all times. You can record interviews or capture actuality. Short audio files can be effective on the Web to deliver sounds of dramatic events. These files are also easier to download and post than video. Remember to get plenty of storage space on your recorder—seek a minimum of 1 hour in high-quality form, and up to 4 hours in lower quality. Remember also the value of images to jog our memory, so take lots of photographs with your portable digital camera. It costs nothing because you're not using film, but the images, no matter how blurred, may help you remember vital information. Know how to set your phone's ringer on silent if you have to attend meetings. One of the keys to being a multimedia journalist is knowing the potential of your tools and how best to use them. As ever, training remains important.

Communicate constantly with your assignment editor or newsflow manager. Remember to ask them what they need in terms of images and audio. Think of yourself as their eyes and ears. These editors and managers are in constant contact with the newsresourcer or librarian, so they often have a better idea of the overall picture.

Your aim should be to avoid producing print, broadcast, and online versions of a story that tell the story in the same way. Always think in terms of the strengths of each medium, and how best to use those strengths for the stories you plan to tell. The best convergent journalism offers the audience a variety of complementary, not repeating, information on a variety of platforms. Brainstorm with colleagues before reporting on a story so that you can hear their ideas on how to tell it. If collaboration isn't possible, mind maps are useful tools for organizing your ideas and generating new ones. See the books of Tony Buzan such as *Use Your Head* (1989) for more information. Remember, you are either expanding or contracting. This is one of the most exciting times to be a journalist.

Journalist and educator Jane Stevens (2002) believes that convergence and multimedia will change "the face, heart, and guts of newsrooms" during the next 20 years. In the early 21st century, would a news executive consider hiring a reporter who did not know how to use a computer, she asked rhetorically. A decade from now, she said, they would similarly not hire anyone who could not "slide across media." The Tribune Company's Howard Tyner believes that journalism's future lies in the area of multimedia, and "we need to embrace it" (2004). Technology will continue to produce innovations that consumers like, and editorial managers have to learn to deal with change. In terms of multimedia, he said, journalists needed to jump on the bandwagon "in a smart way before somebody else does it and has us for lunch in the process."

References

Broadcast Engineering (2004, February 18). "Video journalists extend reach of BBC without adding costs" in *News Technology Update*. Retrieved 27 April, 2005, from http://newstechnologyupdate.broadcastengineering.com/february_18/

Buzan, T. (1989). *Use your head*. London: BBC Books.

Myles, P. (2004, September 1–3). E-mail interviews.

Grant, A. (2004, September 9). Comments noted at Newsplex training, Columbia, South Carolina.

Northrup, K. (2004, September 9). Comments noted at Newsplex training, Columbia, South Carolina.

Papper, R. (2004, November 17). Interviewed in Muncie, Indiana.

Paul, N. (2004, November 12). Interviewed in Los Angeles, California.

Stevens, J. (2002, February 4). Backpack journalism is here to stay. *Online Journalism Review*. Retrieved September 2, 2004, from http://www.ojr.org/ojr/workplace/1017771575.php

Stone, M. (2002, February). The backpack journalist is a "mush of mediocrity." *Online Journalism Review*. Retrieved September 2, 2004, from http://www.ojr.org/ojr/workplace/1017771634.php

Thelen, G. (2004, March 5). Interviewed in Tampa, Florida.

Tyner, H. (2004, October 12). Telephone interview.

Web Sources

American Press Institute: http://www.americanpressinstitute.org
The Media Center: http://www.mediacenter.org
The Newsplex: http://www.newsplex.org
The Poynter Institute: http://www.poynter.org
The Reynolds Foundation: http://www.dwreynolds.org

1 Find a story you think should be covered in your area and do so. Write a print story (500 words), a broadcast reader (25 seconds), and an online piece on this topic. Make sure that you are fitting the style and format of each medium. Also make sure you aren't being redundant. Also, in a short paper, discuss how you would tell the story visually and online. Include how you would augment your work with images, video, audio and interactive elements.

2 Videotape a television news package of about 90 seconds. Transcribe the tape. Discuss what is missing from the story and how you would elaborate on that story if you produced print or online versions.

Football fans watch a "balloon glow" at the east side of the Hickman High School football field during a game on Friday, November 7, 2003, in Columbia, Missouri. (Photograph courtesy of Amanda Goehlert.)

Multimedia Advertising

The beginning of the end of traditional mass media advertising came in February 1993. The first Internet browser, called Mosaic, was introduced and the World Wide Web was soon upon us all. Society and advertising would never be the same.

The creation of the Web and other digital technologies allowed consumers to start taking control of information and entertainment. No longer could the providers of media control what you read or viewed by what they chose to publish or broadcast. Advertising, which serves as the primary revenue source for mass media, started to see its impact on the American media consumer begin to erode.

When Larry Light, the global chief marketing officer at McDonald's, said, "mass marketing today is a mass mistake," advertising people took notice (Ciociola, 2004). McDonald's used to spend two-thirds of its ad budget on TV. Today it's one-third.

The age of traditional mass media is quickly coming to a tipping point. The mass audiences of the past 50 years, driven primarily by TV viewing, are becoming the niche audiences of the 21st century. The one-size-fits-all approach of mass media doesn't fit in today's personalized media world. Video games, cable TV, the Internet, cell phones, blogs, instant messaging, and other digital technologies integrate better into people's lives. The disruptive media of the past are giving way to personally invited media.

In the future, advertising's success will rely increasingly on finding smaller and smaller niches of customers. The era of digital technology is forcing advertisers to seek and find new, evolving forms of media. The winners will target the few, not the many, for their success.

In this chapter you will discover how media convergence is forcing advertising to evolve from mass media to niche media. We'll look at a short history of advertising, the numbers game in advertising, how the Web has changed advertisers' outlook, and the future of advertising.

Advertising Defined

Before we can understand how mass media advertising is changing, it's important to understand the traditional definition of advertising and how it's evolving. In the past, an advertising message had to be:

1. A nonpersonal communication
2. Paid for by an identified sponsor
3. Sent through mass media
4. Meant to inform or persuade
5. Delivered to a target audience
6. About products, services, or ideas

During the decade since the Web was introduced, the definition of advertising has changed as multimedia options have grown. For example, a personal communication may be sent through targeted micromedia, such as cell phones, in an attempt to build brand relationships among a community of users.

The transition from mass media to microtargeted multimedia has greatly accelerated. The Internet has had a major impact on how, where, and when people choose to get their information and entertainment. The Internet has become a "digital queen bee," credited with creating and popularizing many forms of advertising. E-mail, search engines, chat rooms, blogs, online games, instant messaging, and Webcams are new media that evolved from the Internet and are places where advertising messages can be delivered.

As new media audiences grow, companies are shifting their advertising budgets away from traditional TV-based mass media toward a more targeted, multimedia approach. This microtargeting is an attempt by marketers to build long-term brand relationships by embracing customer individuality and catering to the individual's wants and needs. Companies are no longer just trying to sell products or services; they are instead selling life experiences.

A Little Bit of History

Advertising in the form of images, words, or signs has been used to sell goods and services for hundreds of years. In the United States, newspapers and magazines began running classified-type advertisements in the 1700s. Posters, the forerunner of today's billboards, were used in the mid-1800s by P. T. Barnum to hawk his circus. Modern advertising, from about 1870 onward, mirrors the growth and prosperity of the Industrial Revolution.

From 1870 to 1900, the U.S. population nearly doubled, growing from 38 million to nearly 76 million. The economy following the Civil War grew at a rapid pace, continuing into the early 1900s. Several inventions, including the telephone, photography, color printing, the automobile, motion pictures, and the phonograph, helped spur U.S. economic growth and motivated millions of rural families and foreign immigrants to migrate to cities to find jobs. These new urban consumers demanded goods and services and information about how and where to buy them. Modern advertising was born.

At first, newspapers and magazines were the main media options for advertisers. The major consumer companies of the day, including Coca-Cola, Procter & Gamble, Kellogg's, and Sears and Roebuck, used national magazines to educate consumers about their new products. Retailers used newspapers to sell the products locally. Catalogs also became popular, especially to farm families who could order goods and have them delivered to their door.

This explosion of new products and advertising brought with it several ethical challenges. One of the most heavily advertised products at the turn of the century was patent medicine. The elixirs and tonics offered miraculous cures for everything from baldness to gout. Most were nothing more than 80-proof liquor with added flavors. Advertising became the scapegoat for this fraud and gained a reputation for misleading consumers.

165

The government stepped in and created the Pure Food and Drug Act in 1906, protecting consumers by regulating advertising against false claims of medical benefits. It was an inauspicious start for a new form of paid communications that would forever be subject to regulators' and public scrutiny.

A New Electronic Mass Medium Is Born

Radio became the first electronic mass medium, evolving in the 1920s from the wireless technology that was first used to communicate with ships at sea. By the end of the Roaring '20s, radio was on its way to becoming the dominant medium of the time.

The Great Depression thrust radio into its role of media prominence, partly because it was the first "free" media. With unemployment rates hovering near 20 percent during much of the 1930s, many families couldn't afford to buy newspapers or magazines. In contrast, once a family purchased a radio, it had access to unlimited free entertainment and news via the airwaves.

It was during radio's golden age in the 1930s that advertising was able to expand beyond its print heritage. A new form of advertising—the commercial—was developed for radio and became the key revenue source for the medium. The term *soap opera* was coined as a result of the advertising by Procter & Gamble, which used radio programs to sell laundry soaps to housewives.

During the same period, highways began to roll across the country, making billboard and roadway signs an effective advertising medium. With new roads and reliable transportation, families could travel greater distances. Billboards told these travelers about motels, gas stations, restaurants, and tourist locations along the way.

At the New York City World's Fair in 1939, a new technology was introduced to the public that would revolutionize advertising and change media usage forever. Broadcast television's debut was less than spectacular by today's standards. Hazy black-and-white images showing visitors to the RCA TV exhibit were broadcast to a few hundred people who had TV receivers in New York. It would be two more years before TV became an advertising medium.

World War II delayed the growth of television into America's households, but by 1946, the postwar Baby Boom was under way and TV began entertaining a recovering nation. TV helped growing families learn about new products, much like print advertising had done in the late 1800s. In time, TV would become the most dominant mass medium of its time and advertising would be the sole economic force behind its growth. Consumers had adopted no other media as quickly as they adopted TV. In 1950, only 10 percent of homes had TVs. By 1956, that figure grew to 67 percent.

TV's success was a threat to radio and movies. Because TV was initially considered radio with moving pictures, many large advertisers switched their budgets from radio advertising to TV. Movie audiences also declined because TV was perceived as being free and many movie stars became TV stars. Advertisers were quick to realize the potential of reaching millions of homes with one medium. Early TV ads were sponsorships by companies that demonstrated new products, like washers and dryers. It wasn't until the "Creative Revolution" in advertising began in the late 1950s that the 30-second commercial became popular.

From a cultural standpoint, advertising reflects the society of the times. During the mid-1950s, most advertising reflected the straightforward, button-down mentality of the Cold War era. Political realities were reflected in the hard-sell approach used to market products. It was called the scientific approach to advertising. Repeat, repeat, repeat the message was the mantra of advertising agencies. TV was the perfect mass medium for that mantra.

167

In the late 1950s, as many teenage Baby Boomers began to question authority and a new form of music called rock 'n' roll swept the country, advertising began to change. The hard-sell approach gave way to a soft-sell approach, which was more emotional and often irreverent. Humor became a popular way to advertise products.

No mass medium has dominated our lives as long as television. Advertising has been the key revenue source and beneficiary of that dominance. During the peak of TV viewership in the late 1970s, only three broadcast TV networks existed—ABC, CBS, and NBC. An advertiser could have its commercial seen in 75 percent of all homes in the country in one evening by running one ad on those three networks during prime time.

Like the mass media before it, broadcast TV was vulnerable to new technology and forms of communication. In the 1970s, HBO was introduced as the first premium cable channel. Within the next decade satellite TV could deliver new cable channels like ESPN, MTV, CNN, and BET across the country. Broadcast TV's prime-time audiences began to decline.

For advertisers, cable offered the opportunity to target specific viewers that broadcast TV couldn't. Sports, movies, news, and other niche channels drew audiences because of the type of programming they provided. By 1990, 63 percent of American homes were wired for cable and broadcast TV had lost 15 million prime-time households to cable.

Media Advertising: A Game of Eyeballs

As new forms of mass media evolved, so did the need to be able to price and sell ad space to advertisers. The cost of mass media advertising is based on how many people are exposed to an ad. It's called the "opportunity to see." Media providers don't guarantee that people will see an ad when it's run. The providers only guarantee advertisers that the ad will run when and where the advertisers want it to run. It's a game of selling space that has the chance to find the most consumer eyeballs. For newspapers and magazines, ad prices are based on the number of copies produced and distributed. For radio, it's the number of listeners a station draws. The costs of broadcast and cable TV ads are based on the number of households or viewers that watch a program. Outdoor advertising, which includes billboards, street posters, transit bus signs, and wallscapes (huge photos on the side of buildings), is priced by how many vehicles or people pass by a location daily.

The main difference in pricing among media types is the size of the audience, or how many people can be reached by a specific advertising medium. The bigger the audience, the higher the cost. A medium that has a large reach, like TV, is the most cost efficient because it can deliver an ad message to more eyeballs at the lowest cost. For example, one prime-time 30-second commercial on ABC would cost about $150,000 and reach more than 20 million people. A full-page color ad in *Rolling Stone* magazine would set you back about $125,000 and be seen by one million readers. The cost difference is in targeting. Magazines target a smaller number of readers based on their lifestyles. TV uses a shotgun approach to reach as many eyeballs as possible. That's why TV is considered a cost-efficient way to reach a mass audience.

As the number of readers, listeners, or viewers increases, ad prices increase. It's basic supply-and-demand pricing that has worked for nearly a century. Then came cable. As cable TV audiences grew, broadcast TV audiences shrank, but the cost for broadcast TV ad space did not shrink with the audience.

From 1980 through 2003, the percent of households watching prime-time TV on the broadcast networks—ABC, CBS, NBC, Fox,

168

UPN, WB, and PAX—fell from 70 percent to 30 percent. During the same period the cost of running a 30-second commercial during prime time went from $57,900 to $120,500. Millions of people had stopped watching these broadcast channels, yet the cost for ads went up. The same thing was happening with newspapers where readership fell 30 percent in 30 years. In both cases, the "cost per eyeball" was increasing while the number of eyeballs reached was decreasing.

Weaving a Web of New Media

In 1993, the traditional mass media were confronted by a new technology that would dramatically change how people use media: the World Wide Web. Thanks to this technological advance, people could "surf" the Web to find the entertainment and information they wanted when they wanted it. This new media gave people something they didn't have before: control.

With the ability to choose what they wanted to see and when, Internet audiences grew rapidly. It became the fastest growing media of all time. Advertisers didn't wait long to join the party. A year after the Web launched, the first online ad reportedly ran on *Hotwired*. The first ads were static banners, followed soon by buttons and sponsorships. The slow download speeds of dial-up modems didn't allow for the types of interactive ads we see today. Many large companies saw the value of having a Web presence and built sites. The buzz about the Web grew, and with it grew a vision of an uncontrolled, unregulated Wild Wild West of entertainment, information, and commerce.

Today, the Internet has become a key source of information and commerce for people and businesses. Nearly 75 percent of the U.S. population has access to the Internet at home or work, and two-thirds use it regularly. For advertisers, it is becoming the next big media to dominate our culture. Unlike TV, which created a generation of passive viewers, the Internet has grown into a community of interactive users.

Internet advertising revenues were expected to top $9 billion in 2004, up by nearly 40 percent from 2003. At its current growth rate, it could become the third-largest media advertising category by 2010. Several factors make the Internet such an attractive place for advertisers:

- Growing global audiences
- Low ad costs relative to mass media

169

- Pinpoint targeting of consumers
- Accurate measurement of ad investment

The weakness of TV advertising is the strength of the Internet. That's why many large companies, like Procter & Gamble, are moving some of their ad spending from TV to the Web. P&G, the maker of many popular consumer products such as Crest toothpaste, Ivory soap, and Herbal Essence shampoo, used to spend 90 percent of its advertising budget on TV. Today, it's spending less than one-third on TV. Instead, the company is using a multimedia approach to personalized marketing.

A faster Internet has allowed Web sites and advertisers to use more video-based and interactive content. High-speed broadband is now used by more than 50 percent of Internet surfers, opening opportunities for advertisers to use rich-media ads versus the original static banners or buttons. For our ad-weary society, it's a way to add interactivity and personalization to marketing messages.

Searching for Ad Revenues on the Web

Search engine marketing has become an important source of advertising on the Internet. Since the dot.com bust at the turn of the 21st century, online advertising has evolved from ubiquitous banners and buttons to subtle search engine text-linked ads. Thanks in part to this evolution, online ad revenues have soared.

The Web has allowed businesses that can't afford TV or other mass media to market products and services to local and global audiences. Many companies with niche products have found success on the Internet through search engine marketing, the largest segment of Internet advertising. Paid-search marketing allows a company to deliver a message right to the screen of a person searching for specific information on Google, Yahoo!, MSN, AOL, or other search engines.

In 1998, no search engines offered paid ad listings within their search results. As of late 2004, paid search is a $3.9 billion business and accounts for 40 percent of online ad revenue. Advertisers like this approach because it's nonintrusive, consumer driven, and voluntary. In addition, new technologies have been introduced that increase the customization of search requests and help users keep track of past usage. Amazon has introduced A9.com, a search service that allows users to store and edit bookmarks, keep track of links clicked from previous visits to a Web page, and make personal notes on those pages for later viewing.

Google and Yahoo! have introduced mobile search services that allow cell phone users to search the Internet. Both services are focusing on local searches for businesses, such as retail stores and restaurants.

All of these new technologies have one thing in common: They're helping search engine marketing get better and more sophisticated.

E-Mail: The Internet Killer APP That's Getting Spammed

Long before the Web became popular, electronic mail was used on the Internet for communications. The Web, because of its ability to deliver photos, sound, and video, was the ideal place for e-mail to become an advertising medium.

It didn't take long for e-mail advertising to become the first electronic curse of the Web as spam e-mail clogged inboxes around the world. According to Verisign, spam accounts for 80 percent of e-mails.

What promised to be the killer commercial application of the Internet could be in danger of becoming a marketing wasteland if spam is not controlled. The CAN-SPAM Act of 2003 passed by Congress requires that unsolicited commercial e-mails be labeled and include an opt-out option. The problem is that fly-by-night e-mail marketers are hard to catch, so legitimate e-mail marketers suffer as the reputation of e-mail advertising takes a hit.

Many "permission-based" e-mail marketers have found an effective way to counter the scourge of spam. Permission-based e-mail requires that ads or marketing offers be sent only to those people who have signed up and agreed to have a business send e-mails to them.

Making It Personal on the Internet

Online chat rooms, discussion groups, and bulletin boards have made the Internet an intimate and personal medium. They also have given advertisers a place to sell their products and services to willing customers. The Web allowed users to go beyond simple text messages. Photos, video, graphics, and sound could be included in online chats. The Web had few, if any, limits on what could be said or viewed.

Then, as high-speed Internet connections became popular, the use of chat rooms, discussion groups, and video chat became even more interactive. Real-time video feeds became possible, opening up the living rooms—and bedrooms—to voyeuristic Web droolers. Today, Webcams feed live pictures from around the world. There's even a Web site for Webcam locations: http://webcamsearch.com.

Advertisers saw this potential and began targeting high-volume chat rooms with banners and pop-up ads. For many Web sites, chat room advertising is a way to make money to keep the site running. For advertisers, chat rooms and Webcams provide many opportunities:

- Live interaction lets businesses find out how customers feel about their products.
- Entertainment sites are growing as people look for places to get in-depth information about movies, games, and celebrities.
- Web sites that offer chat get more return visitors (remember the importance of eyeballs?).
- Online communities grow around chat rooms because users have the same interests.
- Chat sites can use banner ads and memberships to make money.

Burger King used the power of an interactive Webcam as the basis for its successful "Subservient Chicken" spoof. Visitors could type in a command and watch the chicken perform a live stunt online viewed via a Webcam. As of late 2004, the Web site had received more than 320 million hits from 100 countries, according to bangoncreative.com.

Staying Connected with Instant Messaging

A growing trend is the use of chat with instant messaging (IM). The major IM providers (AOL, MSN, and Yahoo!) have connected chat rooms with their instant messaging services.

Since AOL invented instant messaging in 1999, no other form of Internet communications has grown as fast. Today, there are more than 50 million IM users in America, and more than 200 million around the world. Businesses and consumers are using this simple technology to stay in touch without having to use e-mail or the phone.

For young adults and teenagers, IM has become the cool tech tool. A 2004 study by the Pew American Life & Internet Project (http://www.pewinternet.com) found that 62 percent of adults ages 18 to 27 use IM; for teens it's 74 percent. They keep in touch with family, send photos, play games, and make dates. It's life at the speed of light.

Cell phone companies have been quick to see the opportunities of mobile IM. With a cell phone or PDA, an instant message can be routed through a computer IM service or sent directly from cell phone to cell phone. AOL, the leading mobile IM provider, offers buddy lists and chat rooms via IM.

The largest segment of mobile IM is short message service (SMS). With the push of a button, you can send and receive short text messages between cell phones without having to go through an Internet IM service. Some cell phone services allow you to send and receive messages among all four major IM providers.

Multimedia message services (MMS) is an advanced version of mobile IM service that's popular in the United Kingdom and Europe. It allows for text, video, audio, and images to be sent in messages on cell phones. You can also download ring tones and wallpaper and play interactive games. You can create, edit, preview, and send MMS messages, either via mobile phones or the Web.

For advertisers, IM, SMS, and MMS have huge potential. Being able to send an ad directly to Internet or mobile IM users and have them interact with the message is the ultimate in consumer interaction. It's part of the new multimedia approach using "life flow experience" marketing.

Advertisers around the world are launching interactive ad campaigns using all types of IM. SMS-TV chat lines are a growing advertising source in Europe, according to *The McKinsey Quarterly* (Bughin, 2004). TV viewers of music contests and reality shows can send text messages to vote for their favorite show or contestant. In Germany, viewers can buy CDs and concert tickets on Viva, a music-TV channel.

U.S. Cellular and the Chicago White Sox recently did an SMS text-messaging campaign. During games, the "Question of the Day" appeared on the field's electronic scoreboard. Fans who responded correctly via text messaging were entered into a drawing for White Sox tickets, merchandise, and a chance to "Take the Field" with the players.

In the United Kingdom, 20th Century Fox partnered with a cell phone provider on an MMS wireless campaign for the *Alien vs. Predator* movie. By text messaging ALIEN or PRED to a special campaign number, users voted on who would win the battle between the movie monsters. Voters with color-screen cell phones received free *Alien vs. Predator* wallpaper to display on their phone.

173

The growth of cell phone marketing has been tempered by techno-logical limitations and regulations. Internet or cell phone companies control access to the users. Also, it's illegal in the United States to send unsolicited marketing messages to cell phones or mobile devices. Spim, the mobile cousin of spam, has been kept in check by government regulations.

Let the Games Begin

Online and console games have contributed to the decline of mass media audiences in the past 30 years. From the humble beginnings of Pong in the1970s, the video game industry has grown to become an entertainment powerhouse that threatens a segment of the media audience coveted by advertisers: 18- to 34-year-old men. A recent study by Knowledge Networks/SRI found that these men are playing video games more and using traditional media less. This trend, which began in the 1980s when today's 18- to 34-year-old males were boys playing their first Atari or Nintendo games, shows no signs of slowing. Since the early 1990s, video games have become one of the fastest growing entertainment and advertising media.

In-game ads, which are product placements or sponsorships within a video game, and *advergaming*, in which the game is the ad—think NASCAR—was a $79 million industry in 2003, according to a report from The Yankee Group (Goodman, 2004). By 2008, an estimated $260 million will be spent on these forms of advertising.

Game-based ads can be changed, thanks to in-game advertising net-works like inGamePartners and Massive Inc. Different ads can be run in the same game in different parts of the country or be changed during a game to show different products to a player. This process is called *dynamic in-game advertising*. With the number of console and PC gamers growing to 40 million in 2004, according to Jupiter Research, there will be plenty of eyeballs for advertisers to reach as this new medium continues to grow (Rodgers, 2004).

Being able to download games—and ads within games—to a cell phone is a growing but still untapped market in the United States. The increased use of game-enabled cell phones and other mobile devices should help the mobile-gaming download market grow rapidly in the next few years.

Like many areas of media, a problem with video game advertising is how to accurately measure ad exposure. That was expected to change in 2005 when Nielsen Interactive Entertainment planned to introduce an in-game ad exposure and rating measure. The device will incorporate a watermark—an inaudible audio code—that will show how long and how often players are exposed to product placements.

Blogs Move Mainstream . . . and Mobile

The use of Web logs, or *blogs*, has been a growing Internet phenomenon during the past few years. Anyone with a point of view and access to the Internet sites Blogger, Movable Type, or Radio can build and maintain a blog. As the 2004 presidential election demonstrated, blogs have become powerful opinion makers and reputation breakers.

An estimated 10 to 20 million blogs exist on the Internet, according to blogcount.com, and the number grows daily. Advertisers have followed the growth of the medium and have begun targeting blog sites. Nike, for example, placed its own advertising blog—adverblog—on the Web site Gawker.com to promote its "The Art of Speed" film series. The promotion proved controversial as blogger purists reacted against the commercialization of the art form.

Marketers targeting blogs are finding that site owners are opinion makers with legions of followers, many of whom don't want advertising on the site. To counter this, Blogads, a network of bloggers who accept advertising, was formed. Advertisers, including Paramount Pictures, *The Wall Street Journal*, *The New Yorker* magazine, Gap, and RoadRunner Internet service, have taken advantage of this opportunity to reach bloggers.

An online survey done by Blogads in May 2004 found that bloggers tend to be male (79 percent), between the ages of 31 and 40 (29 percent) with incomes from $60,000 to $90,000 (22 percent). The nonscientific survey also found that 67 percent of blog visitors have clicked on an ad and 37 percent think TV is worthless.

The next generation of blogs, *vblogs* and *moblogs*, is also attracting potential advertisers. Vblogs, also known as vidblogs, vlogs, or vogs, are video blogs that allow users to post video, audio, and pictures, not just text like normal e-mail blogs. Moblogs are mobile phone blogs that give users real-time connections around the world to share and collect photos and messages and comment on life's happenings.

Advertising Grows as New Digital Media Evolves

Digital technologies are offering advertisers new ways and places to target fragmenting media audiences:

- Digital cinema advertising is one of the fastest growing segments of media. The United Kingdom leads the world in cinema advertising, accounting for 60 percent of the $1 billion in global cinema ad revenues in 2003. The U.S. share is 20 percent. New digital projectors allow cinema owners more flexibility in producing ads for national and local businesses.
- Interactive TV (iTV) is finally becoming a successful platform for advertisers. iTV has been successful in the United Kingdom for nearly 5 years. In this country, thanks to the growth of digital TV and broadband Internet, iTV is offering advertisers ways to target families with interactive messages that allow feedback and the ability to purchase products.
- Product placement has been popular in movies and TV for a while, but other less mainstream forms of media are also being used. Domino's Pizza, Red Bull, and Vans recently inked a deal with Comedy Central to embed their products in a new adult cartoon series and video game placements are also growing rapidly.
- DVDs give advertisers interactivity and the chance to leverage promotional partnerships with movies, concerts, and games.
- Online video advertising grew tremendously in 2004. Thanks to the added speed of broadband connections, many marketers are using in-stream ads—video ads shown before you see the online video content—to complement TV ads.
- Interactive kiosks and video networks in malls and retail stores are part of the growing trend toward retail media networks that allow people to get information and interactively shop for products.

Advertisers Evolve to Multimedia

Before the Internet developed into an effective advertising medium, most advertisers used a handful of traditional mass media to market products. National ad campaigns typically included TV and magazines to reach broad national audiences and radio and billboards for local markets. Because audiences were big, using targeted media was not an issue for many products. As video games, cable TV, VCRs, CDs, and the Web gave people other entertainment and information options, companies began to integrate their marketing efforts and use a multimedia approach to advertising. Unlike the one-size-fits-all approach of mass media marketing, multimedia advertising targets users based on their lifestyles and choices of media. It gives marketers better control of the reach of their ad messages and guards against ad burnout. Best of all, it uses various media as building blocks to surround users with the media they choose to use in their daily lives.

Multimedia advertising creates a media multiplier effect that often adds synergy to a campaign. People see or hear messages about a product in multiple places—on the radio, the Internet, at the ballpark, in the mall, on cable TV, and on a cell phone. This integrated multichannel approach gives an ad campaign "lift" or added awareness with its target audience.

How people use media is changing as digital technologies give people more options. A study in 2003 by researchers from the Center for Media Design at Ball State University (http://www.bsu.edu/cmd) found that 39 percent of TV watchers also use the computer at the same time. This trend toward simultaneous media usage is supported by other research that shows people often use two media at once.

The evolution to multimedia advertising in the past decade has been slow because the advertising media industry is so entrenched in the TV-centric mass media model. It wasn't until several large global advertisers began to shift money away from mass media to targeted micromedia that the ad industry began to take notice.

The shift began when P&G, the world's largest advertiser, announced in 2001 that it was moving $300 million of its $1.5 billion U.S. media budget to do a cross-platform deal with media conglomerate Viacom. The deal included advertising in Viacom's TV networks, CBS and UPN; eight cable channels; syndicated TV (think shows like *Seinfeld* reruns and *Wheel of Fortune*); and nonmedia promotions and sponsorships. Since then, many major advertisers have pulled money out of TV and announced cross-platform, multimedia campaigns. Recently, the Mitsubishi Motor Company pulled all of its prime-time network TV ads—$120 million worth—because of high prices and smaller audiences. An American Advertising Federation survey found that advertisers allocated 8.35 percent of their budgets for online advertising in 2004. That number is expected to grow to 17 percent by 2007 (Kerner, 2004).

Most cross-platform campaigns involve using Internet advertising along with other traditional and new media options. What this approach has done is changed how advertisers view all the media options available to them. Instead of using TV and other mass media as individual choices, marketers now look at the toolbox of media available and integrate the best choices into a coordinated plan.

Network and cable TV advertising still totals $60 billion a year, but the trickle of dollars now being spent on multimedia advertising could become a torrent as marketers learn how to get better results through media integration.

Personalized Media: The Future of Advertising

Advertisers can no longer rely on a few types of mass media to reach large blocks of homogenous consumers. Media convergence is giving consumers new ways to access information and be entertained. To reach these fragmented target audiences, advertisers will need to use an optimum mix of new and traditional media to surround consumers with targeted messages.

To be successful, this integration must benefit the consumer, not the media. Consumers are already in control, so advertisers need to react to that. If you want to watch a *Seinfeld* rerun at 2 a.m., media companies should make it easy to do so. Some companies have embraced this need to offer consumer-friendly integrated marketing. Apple's success with iTunes and the iPod show what a marketer can do when it integrates various forms of media to build strong relationships with consumers. The campaigns have included posters, billboards, TV, magazines, e-mail, Web ads, viral marketing, mobile downloads, video-on-demand, promotions, and the rock group U2.

For integration to succeed, new media technologies must allow marketers to reach people as they live their digital lives. Many experts feel that TV and Internet will soon evolve into a lifestyle media device, providing families with access to high-definition entertainment and information, as well as the ability to interact with marketers.

Interactive TV is a quickly growing medium that allows advertisers to microtarget consumers and deliver customized ad messages. With iTV, you'll be able to play online video games, watch any TV program or movie ever made, and talk on your Internet phone as you watch the other person on a live video feed. Advertising messages will be subtly integrated into everything.

This ability to use new technologies to experience media when you want to is at the heart of the evolution in consumer media use.

The Consumer Has the Power

Marketers need to embrace the growing movement of consumer empowerment. The full transition from the old mass media industry to a consumer-centric new media model hasn't fully happened, but it is nearing a tipping point. This revolution is taking place because consumers have changed how and how much they use media. It's driven by many factors, including demographic and ethnic shifts in our population; new technologies that revolve around the computer, Internet, and cell phone; and a desire by people of all ages to be more connected. As media convergence continues, more segments of new media will combine with traditional media and new technologies to enhance the consumer experience and create new avenues for marketing. Consumers will become more resistant to advertising if the way the message is delivered does not fit with their lifestyle.

179

Not all consumers will be able to take part in this new multimedia world. There is a growing Digital Divide between those who can and can't afford the technologies needed to participate with new media. This could slow the total transition to a "post-information society" in which we are defined by the media we consume, not by the products or services.

The mass media culture of the past will eventually evolve into personalized media communities of the future. And multimedia advertising will lead the way.

References

Bughin, J. (2004). Using mobile phones to boost TV ratings. The McKinsey Quarterly. Accessed April 29, 2005, from: http://www.mckinseyquarterly.com/article_page. aspx?ar=1432&L2=17&L3=66

Ciociola, M. (2004). He's lovin' it. How a savvy adman from NY found happiness selling burgers with a clown from Chicago. Philadelphia Ad Club Web site. Accessed April 29, 2005, from: http://www.phillyadclub.com/staticpages/index. php?page=20041109165324899

Goodman, M. (2004). Video games will generate nearly $260 million in advertising revenue by 2008, Says Yankee Group. Yankee Group news release accessed April 29, 2005, from: http://www.yankeegroup.com/public/news_releases/news_release_detail.jsp?ID=PressReleases/news_10182004_mes_2.htm

Kerner, S. (2004). Online media spending expected to double by 2007. Clickz. Accessed April 29, 2005, from: http://www.clickz.com/stats/sectors/advertising/article.php/3432571

Rodgers, Z. (2004). The rise of the game titans. Clickz. Accessed April 29, 2005, from: http:// www.clickz.com/features/insight/article.php/3366051

For Further Reading

Bianco, A. (2004, July 12). The vanishing mass market. *BusinessWeek.com*. Available from http://www.businessweek.com/print/magazine/content/04_28/b3891001_mz001.htm?chan=mz&

Cappo, J. (2003). *The future of advertising: New media, new clients, new consumers in the post-television age*. New York: McGraw-Hill.

Carat Interactive. (2002). The future of wireless marketing. Available from http:// whitepapers.zdnet.co.uk/0,39025945,60027102p-39000544q,00.htm

Donaton, S. (2004, October 18). Adjusting to the reality of a consumer-controlled market. *AdAge.com*. Available from http://www.adage.com/news.cms?newsId=41759

Kaye, B., & Medoff, N. (2001). *Just a click away: Advertising on the Internet*. Boston: Allyn and Bacon.

Stengel, J. (2004, February 12). The future of marketing. *PG.com*. Available from http://www.pg.com/news/management/speech.jhtml?document=percent2Fcontentpercent2Fen_USpercent2Fxmlpercent2Fnewspercent2Fnews_feb122004_execuitive_speeches_stengle_marketing.xml

Web Sources

AdAge: http://www.adage.com
Big Research: http://www.bigresearch.com
BlogAds: http://www.blogads.com
Carat Interactive: http://www.caratinteractive.com
Cellular News: http://www.cellular-news.com
Center for Media Research: http://www.centerformediaresearch.com
ClickZ Network: http://www.clickz.com
DoubleClick: http://www.doubleclick.com
Forrester: http://www.forrester.com
Gaming Age: http://www.gaming-age.com
Hotwired: http://www.hotwired.com
iMedia Connection: http://www.imediaconnection.com
Jupitermedia: http://www.jupitermedia.com
Magazine Publishers of America: http://www.magazine.org
MarketingProfs: http://www.marketingprofs.com

The Media Center: http://www.mediacenter.org
Media Life: http://www.medialifemagazine.com
MediaMark Research: http://www.mediamark.com
MediaPost: http://www.mediapost.com
Mediasmith: http://www.mediasmith.com
Mobile Marketing Association: http://www.mmaglobal.com
MultiMediator: http://www.multimediator.com
Radio Advertising Bureau: http://www.rab.com
Reveries Magazine: http://www.reveries.com
Search Engine Marketing Professional Organization: http://www.sempo.org
SearchEngineWatch: http://www.searchenginewatch.com
Spam Laws: http://www.spamlaws.com
Verisign: http://www.verisign.com
The Yankee Group: http://www.yankeegroup.com

1 In a short paper, explain how media advertising has changed during the past century. What new technologies have changed how people use media? How has the Internet affected the evolution of media? Describe how consumers are involved with the changes in media.

2 Write a few paragraphs that talk about how you process advertising. Do you view TV ads differently than those in the newspaper or in magazines? Have Web ads become obtrusive or do you tune them out? In addition, write a paragraph or two on every medium you can think of and what you think makes for a successful ad in each case.

Firefighters respond to a fire just south of High Street at 12:45 p.m. in Fort Wayne, Indiana. (Photograph courtesy of Will Vragovic.)

Multimedia Public Relations

Changes in technology since the beginning of the information age have provided public relations practitioners with powerful communication tools and unprecedented opportunities to transform the profession's entire approach to relationships. These changes have increased the potential for communication failures by radically increasing competition for time and attention.

The Internet or World Wide Web perhaps best exemplifies the impact of multimedia in public relations. John Pavlik, who directed the Center for New Media at Columbia University at the time, summed up the "good news, bad news" of multimedia use in public relations in a 1996 report:

> Rapid advances in the technologies collectively called the "information superhighway" present both profound opportunities and challenges to public relations and communication management for organizations in the U.S. and around the world. To public relations professionals, the World Wide Web is both a powerful tool of communications and a dangerous threat to organizational well being. Properly used, the Web represents the ultimate communication tool for building relationships between an organization and its publics, both internal and external. Conversely, the Web empowers the individual to create his or her own communication platforms. . . .

Journalist A. J. Leibling once observed that freedom of the press belongs to those who own one. The Web enables everyone to own a digital press. (Pavlik & Dozier, 1996, p. 3)

What has not changed, however, is the fundamental nature of communication. This chapter will attempt to review the most significant advances in multimedia and address their use by public relations practitioners. The fundamental theme we'll work from is the frequently used adage, "The more things change, the more they stay the same."

Public Relations in the Digital Age: What's Changed and What Hasn't

What Has Changed

Digital public relations guru Don Middleberg calls it *Internet time* (2001, p. 18), but however you label it, there can be no argument that public relations in a wired world has to be accomplished rapidly. You all grew up using computers and think nothing of being online surfing the Net while IM'ing your friends, watching cable TV, and talking on your cell phone. All of this instant communication that you find fabulous today will create one of your greatest challenges on entry into the workforce. Your peers in the news business have also grown up with this technology and are comfortable with it. More and more corporate executives are comfortable with it as well. With all these folks understanding how to effectively use multimedia in public relations, it certainly behooves us to maintain pace with advancements in technology.

One of the greatest changes that has occurred in conducting public relations in a wired world is the speed of communication. No longer do practitioners have the luxury of time on their side. "Strategic planning" has almost become a thing of the past.

The news cycle used to be dictated by newspaper and evening news broadcast deadlines. Practitioners usually had several hours at least to track down information once a reporter called to ask questions. Today, as media relations expert Carole Howard notes, the news cycle is no longer expressed in terms of days, or even hours, but in minutes and seconds (2000, p. 10). The Internet has created an instant demand for information, and the demand does not cease with the release of information. The wired environment requires frequent updates.

Among the many social effects of the media studied over the years is the concept of *agenda setting*. Ithaca College professor and former ABC correspondent Chris Harper (2002), who specializes in journalism and digital technology, notes, "agenda setting occurs when editors choose specific types of stories as news and eliminate others, thereby establishing what you should think about" (p. 313). Yet blogs, Web sites, and discussion groups are helping average citizens to understand issues to a far greater degree than ever before. The agenda-setting function of the media erodes almost by the hour. Proof of their waning influence in this regard is the credentialing of bloggers as media representatives at the Democratic and Republican national conventions in 2004. The wired world opens many affordable communications channels to everyone, leveling the playing field and reducing the impact of the media's agenda.

This same democratization of information also increasingly empowers individuals to a degree never before seen in our society. The Internet gives anyone, anywhere, the opportunity to pull information together in any way they want, free from others' interpretations. This environment makes it essential that public relations practitioners provide clear information that can only be interpreted one way. Effective message design is crucial because individuals are getting fewer cues from other sources to guide their thinking.

The convergence of media has created a more vertical media environment for public relations practitioners. The multibillion-dollar partnership of AOL-Time Warner offers one example of the tremendous change this media convergence is visiting on communication. Integrating cable, Internet, broadcast news, and print media into one organization provides us with the opportunity to communicate our messages to a virtually unlimited public. The potential that our message will be carried on overlapping channels provides us with a much greater chance of reinforcing what we are saying than in the past. Corporate media convergence has provided us with the opportunity to reach more people, more quickly than ever.

The other side of this equation, though, creates the scary possibility that we may be shut out of these media channels. The power of these media conglomerates to say "yes" or "no" to your communications creates the real possibility that practitioners could be coerced into reshaping their messages into a form more palatable to the media organization.

Multimedia provides us with far richer message channels, lending greater robustness to our communication. Greater interactivity also provides us with many of the most salient characteristics of inter-personal communications. There is more of a sense of face-to-face communications in a greater variety of message channels than before. This interaction touches more of our senses, giving us more two-way communication and the very real sense of dialogue and relationship building for the long haul.

It's already apparent that the changes in technology dictate that communications is an ongoing process rather than just a collection of tactics. The diversity of media outlets argues for a greater strategic role for the practitioner and the shedding of the tactician role. Practitioners are moving more toward a thinking and planning role and away from a "doing" role. In this vein of thought is the forecast that public relations practitioners will move from "firefighters to crisis managers" (Lattimore et al., 2004, p. 386). Practitioners are also shifting away from short-term gains and manipulation to long-term relationship development along with understanding, negotiation, and compromise.

All of this new technology has also provided more opportunities to do things that, while not illegal, are certainly on the margins of ethical conduct. Therefore, the need to stress ethics in public relations is also greater than ever before. Marilyn Laurie, president of Laurie Consulting and Ball State University's 2004 Vernon C. Schranz Distinguished Lecturer in Public Relations, spoke of creating a climate of trust while at the helm of AT&T's public relations efforts that is particularly applicable to us today. Her philosophy mirrors that of Arthur W. Page, who served as vice president of public relations for AT&T from 1927 to 1946. This philosophy dictates that AT&T should conduct its public relations as if the entire company depended on it.

In the past, the goal of public relations practitioners was usually to ensure that information on the organization was both accurate and timely. Today, the need for complete transparency is essential to ensure our target publics have the necessary information to make informed decisions. With the enormous number of message channels available today, the practitioner who is able to create an open atmosphere and a free flow of information will be the one viewed as most credible.

While many of the writing and design principles for two-dimensional publications and broadcast outlets remain the same, writing and designing for multimedia also requires us to think a little differently. Multimedia delivers messages through a combination of text, sound, and images, so our writing has to address the needs of print, broadcast, and online media. Complex subjects need to be broken into smaller chunks and presented in a layered fashion. However, we must design these chunks in such a fashion that our audience can follow the path in a linear fashion or via multiple entry points. Because they can enter our paths in so many ways, we must design the environment so they can easily return to the beginning.

The ultimate goal of multimedia writing and design is to create an atmosphere that mimics the face-to-face environment. We've got to change our mind-set about writing and designing from an informational approach to an approach that fosters meaningful connections without forgetting the informational role of public relations.

What Has Not Changed

All of the changes just discussed haven't altered the fundamental role of public relations: to build and maintain mutually beneficial relationships. In some ways, this immediate communication actually helps these relationships. The ability to connect directly and constantly with our target publics enhances our ability to maintain positive relationships with them.

Likewise, the underlying theories of communications remain intact despite the vast changes in technology. Theories grow as we add to our body of knowledge, but the foundations of communication continue to hold true. This may be the quintessential area that highlights the proposition of this chapter that "the more things change, the more they stay the same."

The public relations practitioner needs to continue to enter every endeavor with research. This first step in the public relations process remains truer today than ever before. The multimedia environment merely allows us to do faster and more in-depth research.

Flexibility remains the order of the day. The practitioner has always needed to be able to react quickly to change, but today it's necessary to do so immediately as the changes occur. Communicating with constituents needs to be almost immediate, especially in times of crisis. One quick way to give rumors and bad information a solid footing is to be behind the curve in responding.

Public relations practitioners need to be aware of their environment. Known in some circles as "environmental scanning," the essential skill of knowing what's going on around you allows you the opportunity to put things into context and see the big picture. Given the pace of change today, the ability to take a strategic view will allow you to make

189

changes on the fly, with a better-than-average chance the changes will be correct.

The need for access to top decision makers is probably more important than ever. Along with being able to see the big picture, access to the top decision makers allows the practitioner to help guide the organization's actions at the front end and more clearly articulate its actions at the tail end. Without this action, we simply become technicians, a function anybody can perform with minimal training.

It is absolutely imperative today that public relations practitioners engage in ethical conduct. The speed and reach of communications today means any unethical conduct is both known more quickly and known more broadly. Therefore, we have to remain hypervigilant in our role as both advocates for our organization and as minders of public trust. Some use the term "corporate conscience," but however this function is labeled, it is our job to ensure that our organization not only espouses ethical principles, but also matches those words with actions. As the Arthur W. Page Society notes in its principles derived from the practices of its namesake, we must "tell the truth" and "prove it with actions" (Block, 2003, pp. 5–9).

Credibility has always been the foundation of public relations. In this multimedia era, without credibility the public relations practitioner is little more than flotsam in a sea of cyber-debris. The ability to provide unfiltered information to our target publics gives us a greater capacity to build the credibility of our organizations. Sustaining our credibility remains as important as ever, but is also aided by the vast network of media available to us.

Using Multimedia to Build Relationships

Today's environment has changed the way we communicate, but not the basic role of public relations. While the profession continues to debate an exact definition, at its most basic, public relations is the art and science of building and maintaining mutually beneficial relationships. Whether the intent is to inform, influence, or alter behavior, the foundation of the effort is created through the relationship we have with the intended audiences. Used properly, multimedia offers today's practitioner many opportunities to create and enhance these relationships.

Most discussions of multimedia start with the Web. In public relations, the Web allows us to communicate directly with target audiences. As previously mentioned, the Web has enabled our constituencies to receive information directly. This ability gives today's practitioner unprecedented opportunities not only to build relationships, but also to foster trust in the organization.

This also means that the practitioner must accept added responsibility for structuring the communication in a manner that eliminates confusion on the part of the receiver. Despite some protestations to the contrary, the news media can be helpful in putting things into context. This role now falls to the public relations practitioner, who must work harder to ensure all communication is clear and concise. As pointed out in Chapter 3, the ability to write clearly has become even more vital.

Practitioners truly committed to establishing mutually beneficial relationships will seek every opportunity to add value to their organization's Web site. Providing links to all sides of an argument increases the credibility of the site. Likewise, providing links to more in-depth information gives the visitor the ability to become completely conversant on an issue.

Multimedia communication lets the practitioner establish a dialogue. Multimedia technology very rapidly established itself along the "pull" axis as opposed to the "push" axis. This means the practitioner needs to provide as much information as possible, allowing the target public to gather information when and where they wish. If we concentrate on "pushing" information to these audiences, as in the one-way asymmetrical model of communications, we will surely alienate them or annoy them.

191

We are able to enrich the process for both parties by using technology to provide our target publics with better information on an issue affecting our organization. These groups then become more informed and feel more involved, allowing us to gain valuable and continuous feedback on the image and reputation of the organization. This dialogue also gives us the chance to interact in areas of mutual concern, which in turn contributes to better relationships.

The dialogue can be enhanced by any number of blogs associated with the issue. Blogs are becoming more pervasive every day and usually carry with them a cachet of independence that enhances their credibility. Learning how to engage in this new form of dialogue will continue to be a challenge for the practitioner for years to come.

The distance between business and consumer is closing. Time and distance once prevented our target publics from knowing much more about us than what they learned from our occasional mailings. Letters, while highly personal, take days, weeks, and sometimes months to complete the communications loop. The telephone helped close the gap by allowing personal contact, but the telephone isn't always convenient, especially if we play telephone tag.

Web technology, especially e-mail, has created the kind of personal communication that transcends distance and time. Exchange of information is quick, easy, and usually advantageous to the demands of both parties, because each determines when to interact. Critical to this concept is the addition of the capability for our publics to respond directly to us through our Web sites. This probably seems obvious, but you would be amazed at the number of Web sites that do not provide this capability. They pass up many golden opportunities to establish a dialogue with their various publics.

A related, but separate, topic is providing your publics with the ability to "opt in." This has also become a standard feature of more enlightened Web sites, and it is necessary to build solid relationships. It has become bad form for organizations to "push" e-mail to their publics, because it is often considered spam by the receiver. Instead, providing them with the opportunity to decide individually whether to receive information on a continual basis gives control of the relationship to the receiver, which in turn empowers them. You must also make it easy for them to cut the relationship, otherwise you risk incurring their wrath. Angry people can be extremely troublesome to the public relations practitioner because they have quickly moved from latent public to involved public. As public relations practitioners, we should view this opt-in atmosphere as an opportunity to get to know our audiences and empower them to drive our communications initiatives.

The richness of multimedia also allows us the opportunity to customize our communications, creating the sense of having a conversation with someone. The interactive nature of multimedia communications, coupled with instantly personalized messages, produces an environment approaching the intimacy of face-to-face exchanges.

Through long-term exchanges of ideas, the practitioner is able to anticipate issues and make contributions to management decisions. Long-term exchanges with key publics allow the practitioner to gain an insight into the organization's operating environment that few others have the ability to gain. Using this knowledge to provide context for a decision is invaluable to an organization. The long-term nature of the relationship gives the public relations practitioner a greater understanding of the nuances of an issue and how decisions will be perceived. To our target publics, these exchanges are not costly in terms of resources or time. Coupled with the speed of multimedia interactions, these exchanges provide for far more voices in terms of the conversation, enabling the practitioner to have a finger on the pulse in terms of reaction to the organization.

A multimedia approach to public relations that includes the characteristics above allows for what is known as *viral communications*. As the organization opens a dialogue with its various publics and provides added value to them through its Web site, the credibility and integrity of the organization grows like a virus. Friends tell friends, allowing the solid relationship to expand exponentially. Several political candidates have used this technique to their advantage. Few pundits believed that Howard Dean had a shot at being a contender in the 2004 presidential election, but his viral campaign moved him ahead of everybody—at least until he self-destructed in Iowa.

The ability of multimedia communications, particularly the Internet, to allow scattered groups to unify into new alliances presents both opportunity and challenge to the public relations practitioner. The amount of data available on the Internet allows users to become experts on an issue if they are willing to invest some time. Listservs, electronic bulletin boards, and discussion groups allow individuals with shared interests to create synergy of effort. While more highly developed in Europe than the United States, SMS (short message service or text messaging) connects us instantaneously and allows groups to develop and execute strategies at multiple locations simultaneously. The smart public relations practitioner engages these groups to provide perspective and gain better understanding of the issue. The practitioner who lags behind or ignores these new alliances is in for a rough time.

Using Multimedia to Communicate with the Media

A multimedia environment gives modern public relations practitioners a big advantage over practitioners of past decades by allowing us to provide information to all media simultaneously. In the past, the linear nature of batch faxing or phone calls inevitably gave media outlets at the top of your list an advantage. Today, multiple sources receive your information at the same time, leveling the playing field.

This multimedia, nonlinear approach proved worthwhile for your author while he headed the public relations efforts for U.S. European

Command from 1999 to 2001. At that time, he was responsible for all U.S. military public relations needs in 91 countries across Europe, the Middle East, and Africa. News releases on routine military operations were posted to the European Command Web site and distributed to media who had decided to participate by way of our opt-in e-mail distribution method called a *listserv*. Often, a majority of interested news organizations would report the operation solely on the basis of the information provided by our Web site or the listserv, freeing us to serve a wider range of media interests.

The Internet and listservs are only a few of the multimedia opportunities available to the public relations practitioner today. Technologically aware practitioners can use many other methods to distribute news, including Web casting, audio- or videoconferencing, online discussion forums, and text messaging. This allows us to distribute multimedia packages that enrich the story. Text messaging allows us to continuously update important media contacts instantaneously.

While technology is great, we must continue to understand the media's needs. Not all newsrooms are "wired" and some reporters still prefer to receive material by phone or fax. Those reporters who are technology savvy may have special format requirements. Firewalls in some organizations may restrict the size of files that can be sent electronically. Anti-spam software may prevent reporters from receiving your e-mail communications. Webcasts and audio- and videoconferencing may not be possible, especially with smaller media outlets still using dial-up connections. Today's practitioners have to do even more homework to ensure they have a complete understanding of their contacts' working environments.

Regardless of the environment, we have to make it easy for the media to tell our story. One size doesn't fit all, despite the merging of outlets into media conglomerations. Even if newspapers, magazines, television, and radio share a geographic location, each must be treated differently. In the converged world, more effort is required to understand formats, deadlines, and points of contact. The public relations practitioner must understand all of these requirements.

In working with the media in a wired world, it's important to understand the connection between the immediacy of information, context, and trust. Journalists today turn first to organizational Web sites for information. This has fundamentally changed the public relations approach to breaking news. As early as 1999, we practiced a "Web first" philosophy at U.S. European Command. Today, that is nearly a universal imperative, and the information on the site must be continuously updated to remain effective.

At the same time, we must provide context for this information. We must build context into any system or process, especially since many audiences other than the media will be visiting our sites, gathering information, and forming their own opinions. Simply providing information without providing perspective serves neither the needs of the organization nor the needs of our publics.

Finally, the interrelation of immediacy and context inevitably leads to trust—and sometimes the lack of it. Organizations that are viewed as slow to respond, or that try to provide "spin" as opposed to perspective, cannot and will not induce trust. ("Spin" refers to purposefully crafting messages that focus on the positive with the intent to deceive.) On the other hand, those organizations that are both quick and transparent, providing a framework in which to place the information provided, will develop a substantial bank of goodwill and trust with the media. This can provide that extra margin of grace in a time of crisis that can make the difference between the life and death of the organization.

Being accessible has always been a key to media relations, and today's technology makes that possible to a far greater degree than ever before. Lack of accessibility will inevitably lead to lost opportunities and poor media relationships. Wireless communications devices including cell phones, personal digital assistants, and laptops allow for global access any time of the day or night. The downside of this accessibility should be obvious and it is the wise practitioner who works hard at balancing work and life.

We've briefly discussed some of the more obvious Internet uses in building media relations. Let's turn our attention now to a few of the perhaps less obvious uses. Pitching stories has always been an important function of the public relations practitioner. Success or failure in piquing the interest of the reporter or editor rests mainly on the careful construction of the pitch letter. Most journalists today prefer e-mail to snail mail, so this construction becomes even more important. The subject line is crucial and you have to be able to say all you want to say in one "screen," or without making them scroll down to finish your letter. You typically get about five sentences to grab a reporter's interest. The organization's Web site is also crucial, as the interested reporter will undoubtedly seek additional information from your site. This process empowers the media as never before and results in a quicker response and a more mutually beneficial association.

195

The Internet has opened up a whole new realm of research possibilities, too. The possibility to learn of a reporter's interest is instantly available to the practitioner. It is also a much simpler process to come up to speed on opposing views of an issue, which can help the practitioner craft messages that address those concerns. This improves the relationship by facilitating more of a dialogue between reporter and practitioner, which in turn better informs the debate.

Practitioners are turning to the Internet more for evaluation as well. Tracking your organization's media coverage, and that of competitors, tops the list of uses in this regard. Software systems such as PRtrak help take this evaluation to the next level by calculating the return on investment the organization got for its media efforts.

An absolute must for an organization's Web site is inclusion of a newsroom. Crafted with the reporter in mind, the newsroom should include:

- News releases
- Online media kits
- Photos with cutlines
- Speeches and Webcasts of senior organizational officials
- Streaming audio and video B-roll of all manner of newsworthy activities
- Annual reports
- Background materials on the organization, products, or services and senior management
- Archives of all past materials

The materials placed in the newsroom are limited only by your imagination. One caution when placing streaming audio and video on your site: Understand the bandwidth constraints of your audiences. There are still portions of your target publics who do not have the latest technology, and they will not waste hours downloading materials. If at all possible, offer compressed versions.

Many collateral materials produced by practitioners are now available online or on CD/DVD such as media kits, brochures, and annual reports. Again, not all of your target publics have access to or are willing to use the appropriate technology to access these materials. Therefore, it behooves the public relations practitioner to keep paper copies of each item.

More practitioners are taking advantage of Webcast technology to reach a broad audience easily and economically, particularly as greater bandwidth becomes more available. A Webcast delivers speeches, announcements, product rollouts, or news conferences directly to the newsroom. Toll-free phone numbers and e-mail connectivity allow for two-way communications, bringing a similar interactivity to the experience as a live event.

As mentioned earlier, SMS or text messaging offers benefits to the public relations practitioner, especially with regard to breaking news. This multimedia technology allows the practitioner to keep media and other target publics constantly updated.

Another area where multimedia provides the public relations practitioner an advantage is during crisis communications. A solid crisis management plan calls for the use of a "crisis information center" splash page. (A splash page is an "opening title" page that transitions users to the organization's home page. It often works like a magazine cover, alerting viewers to key information.) Keeping the Web site updated means better use of personnel because they are less involved in responding to media queries and available for other tasks. E-mail, text messaging, and cell phones provide for instant communications among the important players in a crisis.

Swissair's September 1998 disaster response perhaps best illustrates the benefits of using technology in time of crisis. "Swissair made use of its Web site as a means of real-time communication on details of the crash" (Center & Jackson, 2003, p. 358). The airline replaced their splash page with information on the accident. They posted 1-800 numbers on the site, as well as links to the latest news releases on the rescue mission. Forms to request passenger information were available and the information was posted in the major languages representing the target publics: English, Swiss, French, and Italian.

Using Multimedia to Communicate with Employees

Management frequently overlooks employees as an important target public, but the smart public relations practitioner understands the major contribution employees make to organizational success. A large body of research demonstrates that an informed workforce is more productive and loyal. Keeping employees informed is also the right thing to do. It's imperative that we redouble our efforts to inform this important audience.

Multimedia technology provides the public relations practitioner with greater capacity and capability than ever to accomplish this important responsibility. The very same technologies outlined earlier in the media section can be brought to bear here as well. The most important element of communicating with our employees is utilizing those technologies that allow for two-way communications. There are, however, several technologies that merit elaboration.

Some in the field of public relations believe that the practitioner is well situated to assist in a new direction of management called *knowledge management*. Lattimore *et al.* (2004) describe the phrase to mean

> "... a collection of practices for getting products out the door faster by better ensuring that all employees have the right information they need at the right time. Knowledge management accounts for the ways an organization captures, stores, shares, and delivers information using appropriate software" (p. 382).

As previously discussed, the Web makes it easy to use, distribute, and share information quickly without time or geographic limits, to provide the right information at the right time. Archives allow for a fuller understanding of the background on the project, product, or process, improving productivity by adding context. Multimedia technology can allow groups to form virtual teams or help subsidiaries to ensure uniform implementation and practice across the organization.

Where the Internet is a vital multimedia tool for the practitioner to inform external publics, the Intranet is a valuable source for informing employees and vendors about what's going on in an organization. It is an essential tool in knowledge management.

Both technologies allow the practitioner to "develop communities of interest, building coalitions and establishing relationships with employees, customers, and other stakeholders," as Jack Bergen, first president of the Council of Public Relations Firms once put it (Lattimore *et al.*, 2004, p. 381). The person in the best position to orchestrate this effort is the public relations practitioner.

Unfortunately, too few practitioners are involved in the organization's Internet or Intranet, leaving many decisions to the organization's human resource managers. This must change if the practitioner hopes to present a unified look and feel for the organization.

E-mail is an extremely effective multimedia tool to effect communication within an organization. However, it should not be used as a "fire and forget" tool. Follow-up is as important as ever, as is using a variety of distribution methods. E-mail should also not be used for lengthy documents. Instead, post the material on the Intranet and send a link to the material in a short e-mail. Don't be like the CEO who sent a 150-MB presentation to all 30,000 employees twice!

We must also work closely with our information technology personnel to ensure anti-spam software doesn't interrupt our communication. As with the media pitch letter, the subject line is crucial to avoid the immediate "delete" reaction. We need to be concise enough in our writing to provide e-mails to our employees that require a minimal amount of scrolling.

Another multimedia option that is frequently overlooked as an internal communication tool is the listserv or opt-in e-mail. It empowers employees to control their own communication needs and ensures that only those publics with an active interest in the subject receive the information. This not only improves productivity, but also stands to create a segment within the organization of highly credible, highly motivated, and well-informed individuals who add immeasurably to your communication efforts.

Employee blogs have the potential to help the public relations effort by providing another valuable resource. An uncontrolled media, this potential resource is only as good as the overall communications effort. Ill-informed or disgruntled employees are not likely to say favorable things about the organization on their blogs, so they cannot be counted on all the time. Neither should they be ignored, because they can help provide the practitioner with insight as to the pulse of the employees. They are also increasingly becoming a highly credible source for the media, which further encourages our attention.

Many employee newsletters are going online today, significantly reducing expenses and publication turnaround. Printing can be expensive, so organizations avoid full-color formats altogether and frequently restrict their publication to four pages. Producing the newsletter online, especially as a PDF (portable document format), allows the public relations practitioner to publish an attractive newsletter without the expense of printing. Employees who desire a hard copy of the publication have only to print out the PDF. We will want to stay alert to how technologically savvy our employees are. To ensure we can still meet the information needs of all employees, we need to keep some hard copies on hand.

Bulletin (or discussion) boards provide an outstanding way to empower employees. Because all employee communication is based

199

on building and maintaining mutually beneficial relationships, this opportunity for two-way dialogue can be helpful to monitor employee morale. It offers the opportunity for the organization to explain policies, provide feedback to employees, and build communities of interest.

Finally, multimedia can be used to communicate with employees during a crisis. Recognizing that employees are some of our most credible spokespersons, it is essential that we keep them updated on all aspects of an accident or incident. Multimedia technology, such as the Internet, Intranet, and e-mail, now offers us the opportunity to keep our internal audience informed at the same time as our external audiences. Senior management and subject matter experts can be made available to explain the organization's response. By monitoring blogs and discussion boards, we can evaluate the effectiveness of our internal communications.

Using Multimedia to Communicate with Communities

Consistent with the theme for this chapter of your text, the role of the public relations practitioner with regard to community relations has not changed. We are still concerned with building and maintaining mutually beneficial relationships between the organization and the community.

Many tactics have proven effective in this regard over the years, including community projects, speeches, open houses, joint advisory boards, and philanthropic contributions. Multimedia has not changed the fundamental nature of these endeavors, but it has allowed for a more robust experience. The multimedia aspect of presentations and activities must not overshadow the content or your communications efforts will not be effective.

Multimedia, especially the Internet and Intranet, also allow you to capture and archive these achievements. Speeches before community audiences can be simultaneously Webcast or audio- or videoconferenced to other constituency groups including shareholders, stockholders, and employees. Preceded by an e-mail with a link to the content on the Internet or Intranet, this content fulfills multiple functions.

Multimedia presentations at special events, open houses, community activities, and the like enhance the experience of the viewer. An organization can use multimedia to tangibly demonstrate that it is socially responsible, a good neighbor, led by dynamic management and concerned participants in the community, and a host of other such intangible qualities.

Multimedia can also be used to tie groups together by helping overcome time and distance problems. A large part of any successful community relations program is the interaction of senior members of the organization with influential members of the community. With the global nature of organizations today, this community typically crosses many miles and time zones making it impractical to invite members of the community to visit the organization with any frequency. Audio- and videoconferencing and Webcasting can overcome these distances, making it possible for these relationships to flourish as never before.

The area in which multimedia helps more than any other is in effectively dealing with activists and disgruntled community members. Multimedia, particularly the Internet, provides outstanding opportunities for the public relations practitioner to connect with groups and organizations in ways traditional media never allowed. It also provides a means for these groups to address the organization directly. As in our discussion on relationship building, multimedia channels such as listservs and discussion forums are helping groups improve their understanding of issues. The smart practitioner uses these very same channels to reach out to activist groups and disgruntled community members to establish a dialogue. This starts a cycle of understanding and interaction that leads to solid long-term relationships.

201

Conclusion

It should be apparent by now that multimedia technology has changed the way public relations practitioners do their jobs. Broader reach and simultaneous communications are key features of this new landscape. It should also be apparent that the principles behind establishing two-way communication and building and maintaining mutually beneficial relationships are as important today as ever. Keeping these principles in mind will help us maximize the use of multimedia technology to accomplish our purposes.

Stretching Stephen Quinn's point in his groundbreaking book, *Knowledge Management in the Digital Newsroom* (2002), to apply to public relations, we must all "work smarter" to manage information and harness technology as a tool (p. 1). We need to adapt to the forces that change the way we communicate, but we must remember that communication is an ongoing process, not just a series of programs or outcomes. We can't simply allow for more voices in the debate and ignore the information this debate provides us. The ongoing nature of the communication process means we've moved past simply trying to persuade and influence behavior into building partnerships and dialogues that have at their root negotiation and compromise. It also means we help our organization best by taking the long view with the relationships we build.

Harnessing present and future multimedia technology to help us achieve these objectives is one of the most important challenges facing modern public relations. With the multiplication of channels and technologies has come a need to understand how and when to use each for maximum benefit. This places a greater emphasis on the research and planning skills of today's public relations practitioner.

Finally, it's important to remember that these new mediums should neither overwhelm nor complicate public relations activities. As long as we don't become slaves to the technology, this new era of communication will enhance our communications efforts and help us build stronger relationships with our publics. As practitioners, we need to use the latest multimedia technology to empower previously disparate and uninvolved groups. We must provide them with the same robust information, opportunity for dialogue, and engagement we provide to more conventional groups. If we are successful in this undertaking, we advance the profession immeasurably.

References

Block, E. (2003). Guidelines for promoting integrity and building trust. In J. A. Kolten (Ed.), *Building trust: Leading CEOs speak out* (pp. 3–15). New York: The Arthur W. Page Society.

Center, A., & Jackson, P. (2003). *Public relations: Managerial case studies and problems* (6th ed.). Upper Saddle River, NJ: Prentice Hall.

Harper, C. (2002). *The new mass media.* Boston: Houghton Mifflin.

Howard, C. M. (2000, Spring). Technology and tabloids: How the new media world is changing our jobs. *Public Relations Quarterly, 45*(1), pp. 8–12.

Lattimore, D., Baskin, O., Heiman, S. T., Toth, E., & Van Leuven, J. K. (2004). *Public relations: The profession and the practice.* Boston: McGraw-Hill.

Middleberg, D. (2001). *Winning PR in the wired world.* New York: McGraw-Hill.

Pavlik, J., & Dozier, D. (1996). *Managing the Information Superhighway: A report on the issues facing communication professionals.* Gainsville, FL: The Institute for Public Relations Research and Education.

Quinn, S. (2002). *Knowledge management in the digital newsroom.* Oxford: Focal Press.

You're the public relations director for a regional health center about to embark on a new capital campaign. In the first senior management meeting to develop a plan of action and milestones, you are assigned the responsibility for preparing the way for the campaign. You are given 3 months before the campaign is actually announced. Provide a detailed outline of a viral community relations campaign using only multimedia that will build the kind of relationships necessary to ensure the success of the program. You may not make mention of the upcoming capital campaign.

You've been hired by a new company selling computer-based training modules to hospitals to develop a media campaign to help boost sales. The company was formed by one of the pioneers of online learning. Write a pitch e-mail designed to interest the major regional daily newspapers in interviewing your client.

You've just been promoted to director of corporate communications for a major glass jar manufacturing company, with overall responsibility for all internal communications with the company's dozen plants worldwide, corporate employees, the North American Delegation, and the packaging branch. You also work with senior management on a wide variety of communications projects and will program all employee communications. At your first board meeting as director, the CEO appoints you to initiate a company-wide quality circle competition. The only guidance you receive is that each plant will hold an internal competition, with the winning team from each plant appearing at corporate headquarters for the final competition. Senior management will leave the details up to you. Using only multimedia, create a detailed outline of an employee communication program designed to introduce this quality circle contest to all of the company's plants.

A small group of friends finish putting on a hole at Eagle Knoll Golf Course in Columbia, Missouri. (Photograph courtesy of Amanda Goehlert.)

Where Do We Go from Here?
Possibilities in a Convergent Future

Soon after the French Revolution started in 1789, the great English poet William Wordsworth penned these memorable words: "Bliss was it at that time to be alive, but to be young was very heaven." He captured the excitement of a watershed period of human endeavors for his audience, but noted that the future belonged to the young. That is the message of this final chapter: that the future is bright for college graduates who are prepared to work hard. Fortune favors the prepared mind. The future is bright for journalists and journalism, and that future offers multiple possibilities for people who are prepared. It helps, though, to pause briefly to look at the past and to see what we can learn from it. As former British Prime Minister Winston Churchill once noted, the person who ignores history is condemned to repeat its mistakes.

The news industry of the 19th century grew because of the availability of some key infrastructures, including steam railways and electricity. These innovations, in turn, boosted the development of the telegraph—the Internet of the Victorian age. Expansion of the railways in the United States and the United Kingdom stimulated the growth of the telegraph. A boom in railway development was a feature of 1830s

Britain, and a similar surge occurred in the United States about a decade later. By the 1840s, British moneymen had invested the equivalent of 10 times the then-value of the country's imports in the rail networks. In the United States, the telegraph similarly followed the rail networks. Samuel Morse's eponymous code—the Microsoft of its day—was first used with the telegraph in the United States in 1844, and it remained the basic form of telegraphic communication for more than a century. Electricity and steam drove commerce and the media. Between the mid-1840s and the American Civil War of 1861–1865, the telegraph transformed American journalism into a news-hungry industry. News became something that was topical rather than what was reprinted from overseas newspapers when they arrived, usually months later.

The news industries of the 21st century are also products of the dominant technologies of the era: the Web, e-mail, broadband, smart software, and third-generation cell phones. The technology is linked by ones and zeros, which serve as the language of the digital world. These advances and a host of emerging technologies will continue to transform journalism during the next decade. Major events such as September 11, 2001, and the Iraq war have also become watersheds in news coverage. The technology used to cover the war and related events such as the Abu Ghraib prison horrors have helped media managers realize the power of digital tools such as small cameras and thumb-sized Flash drives.

On top of all this, we have convergence. In every era, the media industry adapts to cope with changes in society as part of its role of reflecting that society. Newspapers have changed their writing styles, photography has been integrated, graphics have been added, and design has become an element of storytelling. TV news has moved from the "talking head" to on-scene reports and live shots. Online journalists, ranging from those who are tied to high-profile media outlets to those who blog on occasion, are finding and filling niches as well. Bloggers, who are often ridiculed or ignored by mainstream media, are in some ways no different than the new age of sports reporters in the late 1950s and 1960s. Those reporters dug beyond the game story for different angles and varied perspectives on news. Their seasoned colleagues often derided them by calling them "chipmunks," because they were constantly chattering. Yet, these chipmunks, whose ranks included Stan Isaacs, Len Shecter, and Larry Merchant, left an indelible mark on their field as they pushed for more serious and realistic coverage of sports. In each incarnation of news, change occurred and yet news continued to be disseminated. It's often easier to fear change than it is to embrace it. A sign in a friend's office had a Latin phrase that roughly translated to "In waiting, one conquers all." That might have been true in his business, but not in ours. Convergence will wait for no one, so you'd best be ready to go with it.

"The Future" of Media

In February 2004 the chairman of the New York Times Company and publisher of *The New York Times*, Arthur O. Sulzberger, Jr., told a conference at Northwestern University in Chicago that convergence was "the future" for America's media. Sulzberger's vision is one that mirrors an early piece of prognostication by Nicholas Negroponte. In his book, *Being Digital*, Negroponte forecast a time in which people would be able to receive news that they felt was important and filter out all others. Media services would provide what he called the "daily me" for each individual who sought information. This filtered form of journalism would include announcements and news narratives that were focused on the issues that the individual had noted were important to him or her. The information would be sent digitally to the person's home computer and could be perused at that person's leisure. Additional information would be provided as it surfaced (1995).

207

This vision seems elementary now, given the ability to blog, Web surf, and e-mail. We can download information from computers, PDAs, and cell phones. We sign up for e-mail offers at Web sites and receive daily updates from companies and organizations. Negroponte's foresight, however, becomes remarkable when you realize that he made it in the early 1990s, before the explosion of the Internet.

Given the continuing growth of broadband, it is likely that electronic commerce and convergence will far surpass the wildest dreams of people like Negroponte. Early in 2004 the Pew Internet and American Life Project reported that two in five people in the country accessed the Internet via high-speed connections at home. Pew estimated that about 48 million people, or a quarter of all adults, had residential broadband. Among college-educated adults aged 35 and younger, that number had reached 52 percent, Pew said. In August 2004, Nielsen reported that 51 percent of American homes had broadband. Nielsen predicted the number of broadband households would reach 62 percent by 2008.

Broadband makes Web-based convergence possible, because broadband users have a more intense relationship with the Internet and other media than do dial-up users. Gil Thelen, publisher of the *Tampa Tribune*, has noted how people's information-seeking behaviors have changed with these digital improvements. He believes journalists and media organizations need to adapt to those behaviors (2004). Ruth de Aquino, a newspaper manager in Brazil, produced a report for the European Community–sponsored Mudia consortium that showed the public's consumption of news by the start of the 21st century had changed dramatically compared with a decade earlier. (*Mudia* stands for multimedia in a digital information age.) News and information were available on a huge array of devices and formats, de Aquino said. Many other formats had yet to be discovered. The concept of news was changing and becoming more personalized, more service oriented, and less institutional. The consumption of news and information has been increasing an average of 1.5 percent a year since before the turn of the century. American audiences in 2004 were consuming more than 10 hours of media a day. As part of their coping process, people are tending to multitask and use multiple media at the same time.

Changes in How We Work, Not What We Do

What does this big picture scenario mean for journalism students and people recently entering journalism? In some respects, little will change: Clear writing and the provision of context and background will remain fundamental to the journalist's role. So prospective journalism graduates need to be expert with words and know how to write across all media. That has been one of the main premises of this book.

Journalists will also need to embrace the cultural shifts convergence will create. Throughout this book, you've heard a variety of perspectives on how to accomplish tasks that will aid in getting your message across. One issue that has provided a common thread, however, is the issue of working well with each other. Some industry professionals have discussed the "super journalist" or "platypus" model of convergence, but most have called for you to become very skilled in your niche area while still having an appreciation for the work and niches of others. Culture is a hard thing to overcome, because it is often something we use to define ourselves. We categorize ourselves socially by age, gender, education, political affiliation, and other similar demarcations. In journalism, we find ourselves grouping as "newspaper" or "broadcast" or "Web" journalists. While we spend a great deal of time pulling apart the medium-based seams, the truth is that we are more alike than different. To be converged is to respect those differences, but also to celebrate our similarities. We have a common goal of gathering and disseminating information that matters to audiences in varied arenas. To that end, the rest of this chapter takes a big gulp of air and makes some suggestions for you as you prepare for a future in journalism.

The variety of devices for receiving and delivering news will increase. News is already a 24/7 operation, and that process, if anything, will develop in intensity. Convergence means a change in deadlines and attitudes to those deadlines. Ben Estes, editor of one of America's leading Web sites, chicagotribune.com, applies these principles to online journalism through what he calls the Tao of *floid*. His *floid* is an acronym for content that is fresh, local, often updated, involving images and interactive, and aimed at the young demographic. This acronym should apply for all media sites. Let's take a look at the chicagotribune.com site. The day starts at 6 a.m. with overnight content from that day's *Chicago Tribune*, but updates marked with time stamps and update tags soon appear. Local news is provided by *Tribune* reporters and agency copy with local angles. "Our franchise is not Iraq or Washington. It's local news," Estes said (2003). The site concentrates on local content such as utilities, schools, weather, crime statistics, and traffic updates. The site is updated as often as possible. Estes said he wants the audience to perceive the site as fresh. Content varies depending on time of day. The weekday morning concentrates on hard news. At noon, the news is more utilitarian and includes advice on mortgage rates or how to get a better deal on a cell phone. In the evening the focus is more on entertainment. "The stories people see at 9 a.m. are very different from the stories [they see] at 3 p.m. that day," Estes said. Images and a high level of interactivity are integral to the *floid* process, he said, because readers love photographs. They are often the most viewed feature on the site. Interactive features such as polls and message boards are also very popular, Estes said.

209

In this fast-paced world, ethics becomes even more important than ever. Journalists need a strong moral compass, and they need to be trained in good ethical decision making to deal with a changing, fast-paced world. Similarly, skills such as flexibility of mind, a good broad education, a specialist's knowledge, and a global view are essential. You must also expand your view of journalism. If recent research on how journalists view their profession is any indication, one of the few things staunch print and broadcast journalists can agree on is that they've got the best way of telling the news. We sometimes fail to see the limitations of the medium for which we work, mainly because it seems as though we're admitting something is wrong with what we do. This book has clearly outlined that each medium has strengths and weaknesses. Smart journalists in the future will learn to play to those strengths, thus also shoring up those weak points.

While we fail to realize it in many cases, teamwork is not a concept completely foreign to newsrooms. Journalists who interact with other media in an "us versus them" blood feud often overlook the fact that they currently work in a collegial fashion with people who are very different than they are. Print reporters work with photographers every day, as do broadcast reporters. Text is the medium that holds together a newscast, as is the case in a newspaper. A stunning visual image is powerful on television and on the front page of the paper. Again, knowledge and our ability to share that knowledge are two linchpins that connect us all as journalists.

Everything Is Knowable

210

Futurist Esther Dyson has written that digital technology potentially means that everything is knowable. Broadband puts the resources of hundreds of organizations at our fingertips. The challenge, Dyson argues, is filtering what we need to know, ignoring the information and people we do not want to hear from, and finding the best sources of good information. "Instead of finding, the challenge is filtering," she said (2003). This sounds like a job for journalists who are trained to filter and select. Edward De Bono, one of the world's great thinkers, predicted in 1999 that entirely new professions would emerge in the coming decade that involved filtering information: "In the future there will emerge a series of intermediary professions—sorters, digesters, researchers—that will act as a kind of reduction valve," he said. "It is no longer possible for every user to sort through all of the information they want." One consequence of this for some journalists will be a move from newsgathering to news processing as a primary job responsibility. Future journalists will spend as much time each day, and possibly more in some positions, editing and assembling the huge volume of news that arrives at a news organization, rather than gathering it. The need for quality editors—people can who manage large volumes of information—will increase. The role of the journalist as provider of context and background will become even more relevant.

Writing styles may need to change, to accommodate different audiences. For breaking news online, the inverted pyramid form of reporting remains the best way to get information on the Web quickly and effectively. Journalism may evolve into two main forms: very short (breaking news online and news briefs on paper) and very long (magazine-style writing and enterprise or investigative reporting). The latter will likely be valuable when audiences have the time to dedicate to long-form journalism, or in situations where professionals need deep content such as in the pages of publications like *The Wall Street Journal*. Literary journalism is ideal for some of these circumstances, but journalists also need to give their audiences inverted-pyramid stories and bullet points. The skills of synthesis and analysis may involve boiling down a huge amount of data and information into a few hundred words on a single subject. Think of the way *The Wall Street Journal* summarizes the key business and news events in the "What's News" section of its front page, and transfer that format to your local daily or Web site. Sometimes, all that busy people can process is a synthesized form of news.

211

Smart journalists need to think of themselves as content providers in the best sense of the word. Content has never been king because the world already has more than enough content. We know it as data smog and information overload. Quality content is what will keep the media alive and intelligent; educated reporters and editors will help shape and mold this form of journalism. By providing useful, novel, and intelligent content, journalists can keep audiences interested and informed.

As we've reiterated at many stages of this book, the technology continues to boom, but that is just a small part of what will make convergence successful. All the technology in the world can't make you write better, find better images, improve your diction, or work well together. In the end, the success or failure of convergence comes down to the people who either make it work or stand in its way.

Convergence involves recognizing that audiences are changing and that we need to give those audiences what they seek in terms of news and information. This is why, at many stages of this book, we eschewed the opportunity to turn this into a technical manual. We could very easily have written a great deal more about how to use a particular type of software or how use a specific piece of technology. Instead, we attempted to show you how to build the skills of a good journalist and how to use those skills to meet the challenges of operating in a convergent world. This will allow you to continue to grow and adapt to the latest forms of technology as you apply these skills in each new phase of your journalistic growth. Now, whether you take advantage of the opportunities convergent journalism provides is up to you.

References

de Aquino, R. (2002, May). *The print European landscape in the context of multimedia.* Presentation at Mudia (Multimedia in a Digital Age) in Bruges, Belgium. Retrieved March 23, 2004, from http://ecdc.info/publications/index.php

Dyson, R. (2003, November 15). Comments during panel discussion about the future at the Online News Association's annual conference, Chicago.

Estes, B. (2003, November 15). Presentation to Online News Association annual conference, Chicago.

Negroponte, N. (2005). *Being digital.* Hodder & Stoughton, London.

Thelen, G. (2004, March 5). Interviewed in Tampa, Florida.

212

About the Authors

Wright Bryan is a producer at NPR.org, National Public Radio's website. He previously served as the Web news editor for NewsLink Indiana (NLI), a multiple-platform regional news service based at Ball State University. He was brought to Ball State to help create a working laboratory for news convergence, and thus Bryan directed the creation of newslinkindiana.com. This entirely student-staffed operation was honored in its first year as a 2004 Online News Association Awards finalist in the Best Student Web Site category. Bryan continues to help guide NewsLink Indiana, working as an editor, producer, teacher, and writer.

Bryan received a bachelor's degree in history from Tulane University in New Orleans, Louisiana. He worked for five years as a writer, editor, and producer at CNN.com in Atlanta, Georgia, starting in the CNN.com newsroom before moving to the site's special projects group. As senior editor in charge of special projects, he directed production of "Colombia: War without End," which won a 2001 Online Journalism Association Award for enterprise journalism.

John C. Dailey is an assistant professor of multimedia in the telecommunications department at Ball State University. Before landing at Ball State, he was the creative director for the University of Kentucky Media Center for the Future and an assistant professor of interactive media at Southwest Missouri State University, in Springfield, Missouri. Prior to his career as a college professor, he spent more than 12 years working in live television production, serving in every capacity from studio camera operator to electronic graphics artist and on-air director.

Dailey received his bachelor's degree in general studies, a master's degree in communication from the University of Kentucky, and a Ph.D. in communication from the University of Missouri. His primary creative efforts lie in the area of human/computer interaction. In particular, he is interested in the design of multimedia environments that communicate in interesting yet comfortable ways. His creative interests include multimedia interactivity design, Web application development, new communication technologies, interactive storytelling, and VR photography. He is a charter member of the Indiana Usability Professionals Association as well as member of the International Digital Media and Arts Association and the Media Communication Association–International.

Vincent F. Filak is an assistant professor at Ball State University where he teaches undergraduate courses in news writing and graduate courses on media theory. He also serves as the faculty adviser to *The Ball State Daily News*, the university's award-winning newspaper. Prior to his arrival at Ball State, he taught news writing and reporting at the University of Wisconsin and the University of Missouri. He also worked as a night-side city desk reporter at the *Wisconsin State Journal* in Madison, Wisconsin.

He received a bachelor's degree and a master's degree in journalism from the University of Wisconsin and a Ph.D. from the University of Missouri. His dissertation examined how intergroup bias between print and broadcast journalists can create problems for converging newsrooms. He has conducted several studies and has published scholarly work on this topic. He has also published research on media coverage of the September 11, 2001, terrorist attacks and the impact of psychological need-satisfaction on college learning.

Filak serves as a reviewer for the *Atlantic Journal of Communication* and the *Newspaper Research Journal*. He is a member of College Media Advisers, the Association for Education in Journalism and Mass Communication and Kappa Tau Alpha, the national honor society in journalism and mass communication.

Jennifer George-Palilonis is the journalism graphics sequence coordinator at Ball State University and a project director for Garcia Media. At Ball State, she teaches upper-level newspaper design, graphics reporting, and multimedia storytelling courses and serves as the design adviser to *The Ball State Daily News*, the university's award-winning newspaper. She is also the faculty adviser for the nation's largest student chapter for the Society for News Design. As a design consultant, she has worked on the redesigns of more than 15 publications, including *Crain's Chicago Business* and the *Portland Press-Herald* in Maine. Prior to joining the faculty at Ball State in 2001, she was the deputy design director at the *Chicago Sun-Times*, and before that, a news designer at the *Detroit Free Press*.

George-Palilonis earned her bachelor's degree and her master's degree from Ball State. She is the lead author of *Design Interactive*, an electronic textbook on basic communications design principles and concepts. Her research interests include visual rhetoric, media convergence, multimedia storytelling, and electronic textbook development. She is currently writing a book titled *A Practical Guide to Graphics Reporting* to be published by Focal Press in 2006.

Michael Hanley is an assistant professor of journalism at Ball State University, where he teaches advertising, branding, media planning and buying, and mass media research. He has more than 20 years of executive brand management, advertising and marketing experience with two Fortune 500 financial services companies (Lincoln Financial Group and Conseco), a Fortune 500 energy company (Vectren), a national accounting and consulting firm (Crowe Chizek and Company LLP), and an energy systems distributor (WaterFurnace of Indiana).

Hanley, who has a bachelor's degree in visual design from Purdue University and a master's degree in journalism from Ball State, consults on branding, strategic marketing, advertising, and database marketing through his consulting firm, Hanley Communications. He has developed BrandSmart^{TM}, a proprietary brand development process, to help businesses develop, manage, and nurture their brand equity.

His work in brand management, advertising, writing, marketing, and photography has earned him several awards, including an international Telly Award for radio advertising and a Pulitzer Prize as a news photographer at the Fort Wayne (Ind.) *News-Sentinel.*

215

Terry Heifetz is managing editor of NewsLink Indiana, a multiple-platform regional news service based at Ball State University. He also serves as the news director of Indiana Public Radio. His work with NewsLink Indiana allows him the opportunity to work with students in providing a one-of-a-kind news service for East Central Indiana. In addition to publishing at newslinkindiana.com, NewsLink reports can be heard on Indiana Public Radio and viewed on WIPB-TV, East Central Indiana's public broadcasting station.

Heifetz, who earned a bachelor's degree in journalism from the University of Missouri, spent 15 years in the news business before he began teaching Ball State students how to report and produce in a converged news environment. Most recently, he has produced "The Wall Street Journal Report" at CNBC. He also spent time working at The Weather Channel in

Atlanta, KCRG-TV in Cedar Rapids, Iowa, WFTS-TV in Tampa, Florida, WPTA-TV in Fort Wayne, Indiana, and WISH-TV in Indianapolis, Indiana.

Robert A. Papper is a professor in the telecommunications department and head of the broadcast news sequence at Ball State University. A graduate of Columbia College and the Columbia Graduate School of Journalism, he worked as a producer, writer, and manager at television stations in Minneapolis (WCCO-TV), Washington, D.C. (WRC-TV), San Francisco (KPIX-TV), and Columbus, Ohio (WSYX-TV), and currently serves as research coordinator for the Center for Media Design's Local News Project. He is a former chair of journalism at Ohio Wesleyan University and former broadcast news program director at The American University in Washington, D.C.

He is the author of *Broadcast News Writing Stylebook* and has won more than 100 state, regional, and national awards, including 10 regional Edward R. Murrow Awards (most recently in 2003) and a DuPont-Columbia award for "Outstanding Contributions to Television."

He is a past president of the Maine Association of Broadcasters and a long-time member of the national education committee and task force of the Radio Television News Directors Association. He has overseen the annual research for RTNDA for the last 11 years. He serves as associate editor of *The International Digital Media & Arts Association Journal* and editor of *Electronic News: A Journal of Applied Research & Ideas*.

Thomas A. Price is an assistant professor of photojournalism at Ball State University and has served as the photojournalism sequence coordinator since 1997. During his time at Ball State, the photojournalism program has become recognized as one of the top programs in the country.

Price received a bachelor's degree in English from the University of South Carolina and a master's degree in communication photography from Syracuse University. During a 21-year career at *The News-Press* in Fort Myers, Florida, as photographer, picture editor, and director of photography, he was recognized by the Robert Kennedy Journalism Awards (grand prize and first prize, print), the National Headliners Awards, Best of Gannett, Associated Press Managing Editors, National Press Photographers Association, Florida Society of Newspaper Editors, and the Florida Press Club among others. He is listed in *Who's Who in America* and *International Who's Who of Information Technology*.

His work has been published in more than 40 international, national, and regional publications. He also conducts research in the areas of new media and readers' reactions to photographs and design.

Robert S. Pritchard, APR, Fellow PRSA, Captain, U.S. Navy (retired), is an assistant professor of public relations and serves as the faculty adviser for the Public Relations Student Society of America chapter and for Cardinal Communications, the university's student-run public relations agency.

Pritchard completed his 27-year naval career as the director of public relations for the U.S. European Command in Stuttgart, Germany, his third consecutive Unified Command public relations position. In the span of those three assignments, he managed all U.S. military public relations activity in 73 countries, territories, and possessions in the Pacific; 91 countries in Africa, Europe, and the Middle East; and for the nation's strategic forces. Throughout his career as a navy public affairs officer, he was responsible for designing, writing, and producing the full spectrum of publications including daily newspapers, award-winning magazines, and countless collateral and promotional pieces.

He received a bachelor's degree from Phillips University in business administration and a master's degree in public relations from Ball State. His research interests include crisis management communications, issues management, management counseling, and professional development.

217

Stephen Quinn is an associate professor of journalism in the Faculty of Arts at Deankin University in Australia. He previously served as an associate professor of journalism at Ball State University and as both the director of the Center for Media Training and Research and an associate professor of journalism at Zayed University in Dubai in the United Arab Emirates. He has also taught journalism in the United Kingdom, Australia, and New Zealand.

Between 1975 and 1990, Quinn worked full time as a reporter, writer, editor, and columnist in Australia, Thailand, the United Kingdom, and New Zealand. He started with regional newspapers in Australia (the *Newcastle Herald*) and has worked—in chronological order—for the *Bangkok Post*, the Press Association in London, BBC-TV, the Australian Broadcasting Corporation, Television New Zealand, Independent Television News in London, and *The Guardian* in London.

He received his bachelor's degree from the University of Newcastle in Australia, his master's degree from The City University in London, and his Ph.D. from the University of Wollongong in Australia.

Quinn is the author of *Convergent Journalism* and *Conversations on Convergence* (both New York: Peter Lang, 2005), *Knowledge Management in the Digital Newsroom* (Oxford: Focal Press, 2002), *Digital Sub-Editing and Design* (Oxford: Focal Press, 2001), *Newsgathering on the Net*, second edition (Melbourne: Macmillan, 2001), and *The Art of Learning* (Sydney: UNSW Press, 1999).

Tim Underhill is the production manager for NewsLink Indiana at Ball State University, a newsroom designed to teach converged journalism. In his current position, Underhill is responsible for the production of a nightly television newscast using cutting-edge all-digital technology.

He received his bachelor's degree in telecommunications at Ball State and returned to the university in 1990 after several years in television news. He has worked as a video journalist for network affiliates in Rockford, Illinois; Grand Rapids, Michigan; and Indianapolis, Indiana. His work has appeared on several national and regional networks including ABC, NBC, CBS, CNN, ESPN, and FOX. He has covered the Indianapolis 500, Brickyard 400, NBA playoffs, Pan Am Games, NCAA championships, NFL Monday Night Football, and other college and professional sporting events.

He has served as a judge for several video contests including the Emmy Awards, NPPA, SPJ, and other competitions. His work has earned awards from many of those same organizations including NPPA, AP, and the Emmy Awards. In 2001 he received the Ball State Alumni Association's top award for service to the university, the "Benny" Award.

Index

A

Abbreviations, 56
Accessibility in public
    relations, 195
Acronyms, 57
Actualities, 62
Advergaming, 174
Advertising, 163–82; *see also*
    Consumer driven
    advertising; Instant
    messaging (IM); Mass
    media advertising;
    Multimedia
    advertising
  blogs, 175
  and digital media, 176
  evolving definitions of,
      164–65
  exercises, 182
  history, 165–66
  Internet, 169–75
    broadband, 170
    chat rooms and
    discussion groups,
    171–72
    e-mail, 171
    paid search marketing,
    170–71
    Webcams, 172
  overview, 163–64
  video game, 174–75
Agenda setting, 187
Ambient sound, 62; *see also*
    Natural sound; Wild
    sound

Anderson, Mark, 121
Arrow Tool, in FCP, 138
Assignment editors, *see*
    multimedia
    assignment editors
Attribution of sources, 60
Audiences
  fragmented, 8–9
  size of and advertising
    prices, 168–69
Audio for digital video,
    119–21
  microphones, 120–21
  natural sound, 119–20
Autosave Vault setting of
    FCP, 131

B

Background, 41–42
Batch option, in FCP capture,
    133
Billboards, 166
Black and white balancing,
    116–17, 129
Blogs, 75–77
  and advertising, 175
  critique of news in, 76–77
  interactivity of, 76–77
  and news reporting, 76
  and PR for employees,
    199
  special-interest, 77
Body of Web stories, 73–74
Boxes, double, 63–64

Box graphics, 62–63
Brady, Matthew, 101–2
Breaking news, 30–34
Breakout formats, 71
British Broadcasting
    Company (BBC),
    151–52
Broadband Internet, 9–10,
    207–8
  and advertising, 170
  Sulzberger's *New York
    Times*, 10
Broadcast journalism, *see also*
    Radio; Speech and
    writing for broadcast;
    Television
  information graphics in,
    82–83
  versus print, 15, 153–54
Broadcast television
    advertisements,
    167–69
"B" roll, 138–39
Brown, Joe, 15
Bulletin boards, 199–200
Burns, Ken, 106–7
Business models and
    convergence, 14–15

C

Cable television, 167–69
Cameras, professional
    television, 115–16

Canvas Window, in FCP, 135–37
  Fit to Fill Edit command, 136–37
  Insert Edit command, 136
  Jog and *Shuttle Controls*, 137
  Overwrite Edit command, 136
  Replace Edit command, 136
  Superimpose Edit command, 137
  Timeline VTR controls, 137
Capturing, in FCP, 131–34
  Capture Batch option, 133
  Capture Clip option, 133
  Capture Now option, 132
  logging clips, 133
  IN and *OUT* points, 133
  VTR controls, 132
Cellular phones, 173
Chat rooms, 171–72
Chicago Tribune, 209
Child labor, 102–4
Chronological story development, 61–62
Cinema advertising, digital, 176
Circus analogy of convergence, 7
Civil War, 101–2
Clip-on microphones, 120
Clip option, in FCP capture, 133
Cloning, 24–25
Closure for stories, 45
Collaborative editing, 48–49
Commitment statements, 123
Communication
  crisis, 197, 200
  speed of, and multimedia PR, 186
  theories, 189
  viral, 193
Communities and public relations, 200–201

Consumer driven advertising, 178–79
Content, 24–25, 211
Context, 194–95
Contractions in broadcast writing, 59–60
Convergence, *see* media convergence
Convergence continuum, 24–26
Coopetition, 24–25
Copy, fixing, 48–49
Corporate conglomeration, 4
Coverage of news, *see* news coverage
Craft mastery, 153
Credibility and public relations, 188, 190
Crimean War, 100–102
Crisis communications, 197, 200
Critiquing news in blogs, 76–77
Cross-promotion, 24–25
Culture and convergence, 208–9
  intergroup bias dynamic, 15–16
  organizational, 3–4
Cutaway shots, 108
Cuts, 118–19
Cycles, news, 186

D

Dailey, Larry, 5, 6, 24
De Bono, Edward, 210
Decision makers, 190
Demo, Lori, 5, 24, 82
Democratization of photography, 102–4
Design, multimedia, 188–89
Details, in news stories, 46
Dewey, John, 127
Dialogues, 191–92
Difficult convergence, 11–12
Digital media advertising, 176
Digital still photography, 104–5

Digital video (DV), 110, 115–24; *see also* Audio for digital video; Nonlinear editing (NLE)
  audio for, 119–21
    microphones, 120–21
    natural sound, 119–20
  editing, 127–44
    black and white balancing, 129
    overview, 127
    shooting tips, 128–29
  exercises, 124
  image composition, 117–19
    framing, 117–18
    pacing and timing, 119
    pans and zooms, 118
    rack focusing and cuts, 118–19
    sequences, 118–19
    for Web, 119
  overview, 115
  professional television cameras, 115–16
  storytelling, 121–22
    and photographer safety, 122
    steady filming and tripod use, 121–22
    thesis or commitment statements, 123
  white and black balancing, 116–17
Discussion boards, 199–200
Discussion groups, online, 171–72
Documentaries, 106–7
Double boxes, 63–64
DVDs, 176
Dynamic in-game advertising, 174
Dyson, Esther, 210

E

Eastman, George, 102
Easy convergence, 11–12
Easy Setup dialog of FCP, 131

Editing, 47–50; *see also* Nonlinear editing (NLE)
  as collaborative process, 48–49
  digital video, 127–44; *see also* Final Cut Pro (FCP)
    black and white balancing, 129
    Dewey's learning by doing, 127
    overview, 127
    shooting tips, 128–29
  final edit, 49–50
  versus fixing copy, 48–49
  still photos, 105–7
    Burns's documentary techniques, 106–7
    interactivity, 107
    newspapers and magazines, 106
    Web, video, TV, and slideshow, 106–7
  by writer, 47–48
Editorial meetings, 27–28
Editors, *see* multimedia assignment editors
Education, 16–17
E-mail, 198–99
  and advertising, 171
  pitching stories in by PR practitioners, 195
Employees and public relations, 197–200
  blogs, 199
  bulletin or discussion boards, 199–200
  crisis communications, 200
  e-mail, 198–99
  Intranet, 198
  knowledge management, 198
  listservs, 199
  newsletters, 199
Ending stories, 45
Environmental scanning, 189–90
Estes, Ben, 209

Ethics
  and multimedia public relations, 188, 190
  and still photography, 109
Evaluation, public relations, 196
Explorative graphics, 83–85

F

Federal Communications Commission (FCC), 11
Fenton, Roger, 100–102
Film editing, 106–7; *see also* Digital video (DV)
Filtered journalism, 207
Filtering news, 210
Final Cut Pro (FCP), 128–42
  Canvas Window, 135–37
    Fit to Fill Edit command, 136–37
    Insert Edit command, 136
    Jog and *Shuttle Controls*, 137
    Overwrite Edit command, 136
    Replace Edit command, 136
    Superimpose Edit command, 137
    Timeline VTR controls, 137
  capturing, 131–34
    Capture Batch option, 133
    Capture Clip option, 133
    Capture Now option, 132
    logging clips, 133
    IN and *OUT* points, 133
    VTR controls, 132
  sample edit, 138–42
    shooting "B" roll, 138–39
    video footage, 139–40

sequences, 134–35
    Linking and *Snapping* indicators, 135
    Name tab, 134
    Timeline, 134–35
  setup and storage, 129–31
    Autosave Vault setting, 131
    Easy Setup dialog, 131
    Scratch Disks setting, 130–31
    System Settings dialog, 130–31
    Toolbar, 138
    Viewer Window, 137–38
Final edits, 49–50
Fit to Fill Edit command, in FCP, 136–37
Fixing copy, 48–49
Flexibility in public relations, 189
Floid process, 209
Formats, breakout, 71
Formats, story, *see* story formats
Fragmented audiences, 8–9
Framing video images, 117–18
Full convergence, 24, 26

G

Gentry, James, 11–12
Giner, Juan Antonio, 7
Global media convergence, 12–13
Gordon, Rich, 4
Grant, Augie, 155–56
Graphics, box, 62–63; *see also* Information graphics

H

Haile, John, 3–4, 14
Handheld microphones, 120
Hard-sell advertising, 167
Headlines, 71–72
Hine, Lewis, 102–4
Huang, Edgar, 16–17

I

Image composition for video, 117–19
  framing, 117–18
  pacing and timing, 119
  pans and zooms, 118
  rack focusing and cuts, 118–19
  sequences, 118–19
  for Web, 119
Immediacy of information, 194–95
Informality in broadcast writing, 58–59
Information, primacy of, 157–58
Information-gathering convergence, 6
Information graphics, 81–96; see also Multimedia information graphics; Online journalism; *South Florida Sun-Sentinel*
  exercises, 96
  history, 82–85
    broadcast news, 82–83
    print journalism, 82
    role of *USA Today*, 82
  overview, 81–82
  power of, 94–95
  reporters, 86–89
In-game ads, 174
Initials in broadcast writing, 57
IN points, in FCP, 133
Insert Edit command, in FCP, 136
Instant messaging (IM), 172–74
In-stream ads, 176
Instructive graphics, 83–84
Interactive TV (iTV), 176, 178–79
Interactivity
  in multimedia journalism, 148–49
  of still photos, 107
  of Web, 70, 76–77

Intergroup bias dynamic, 15–16
Internet, 185–86; see also Broadband Internet; Online journalism; Writing
Internet advertising, 169–75
  broadband, 170
  chat rooms and discussion groups, 171–72
  e-mail, 171
  instant messaging, 172–74
  paid search marketing, 170–71
  Webcams, 172
Interviews, 42
Intranet, 198
Inverted pyramid method, 43–44; see also Leads
  for Web writing, 70–74
    body, 73–74
    breakout formats, 71
    headlines, 71–72
    importance of text, 70–71
    nut graphs, 73
    shovelware, 71

J

Jog Control, in FCP, 137
Journalism schools, 16–17

K

Knowledge management, 198
Kodak, 102

L

Lattimore, 198
Lavaliere microphones, 120
Leads
  in broadcast, 61
  in print news, 44–45
  in Web stories, 72–73
Learning by doing process, 127
Legal regulation of convergence, 10–11
Linking indicators, in FCP, 135

Listservs, 194, 199
Literacy, multimedia, 153
Live reports, 62, 63–64
Logging clips, in FCP, 133
Long-term public relations, 192–93

M

Magazines, 106; see also Print media
Management, knowledge, 198
Managers, newsflow, 155
Marketing, see advertising
Mass media advertising, 163–64, 166–69
  audience size-based pricing, 168–69
  billboards, 166
  radio, 166
  television
    broadcast versus cable, 167–69
    hard-sell and soft-sell techniques, 167
Mastery, craft, 153
Media, digital, see digital media advertising
Media and public relations, 193–97
  accessibility, 195
  immediacy, context, and trust, 194–95
  listservs, 194
  newsrooms, 196
  pitching stories in e-mails, 195
  research and evaluation, 196
  splash pages in crisis communications, 197
  Webcast technology, 197
Media convergence, 3–19, 147–60, 205–12; see also Advertising; Information graphics; Multimedia assignment editors; Producers

BBC's PDP VJ program, 151–52
broadband Internet, 9–10, 207–8
and business models, 14–15
and corporate conglomeration, 4
cultural factors, 15–16, 208–9
easy and difficult convergence, 11–12
emphasis on content, 211
filtered journalism, 207
floid process at *Chicago Tribune*, 209
and fragmented audiences, 8–9
as future of media, 207–8
Giner's circus analogy, 7
as global trend, 12–13
Gordon's forms of convergence, 4–6
    information-gathering, 6
    ownership, 4–5
    storytelling or presentation, 6
    structural, 5–6
    tactical, 5
and importance of news event, 7
interactivity of, 148–49
legal regulation of, 10–11
multi-skilled journalists, 152–56
    broadcast versus print journalists, 153–54
    craft mastery and multimedia literacy, 153
    quality of work by, 154–55
necessary skills, 156–57, 209–10
    Photoshop, 156–57
    writing, 40–41, 211
news filtering and processing, 210

newsflow managers, 155
newsresourcers, 155
and organizational culture, 3–4
overview, 3–8, 147–48, 205–7
primacy of information, 157–58
producer-driven and reporter-driven stories, 150–51
storybuilders, 155
storytelling and narrative structure, 148–49
survey of journalism schools and, 16–17
telegraph's influence on journalism, 205–6
training for, 149
use of tools, 158
utilizing medium strengths, 148, 158
Media Corporation of Singapore (MCS), 10–11
Media multiplier effect, 177
Meyer, Cheryl Diaz, 105
Micromedia advertising, *see* multimedia advertising
Microphones, 120–21
Middle material in news stories, 46–47
Mobile phones, 173
Movie editing, 106–7; *see also* Digital video (DV)
MSNBC.com, 84
Multimedia
    and still photography, 100, 110–11
    digital video or platypus journalism, 110
    storytelling forms, 111
    and writing for Web, 70, 74–75
Multimedia advertising, 176–79
    consumer driven, 178–79

media multiplier effect, 177
Multimedia assignment editors, 7, 21–36, 150; *see also* Convergence continuum; News coverage
    exercises, 36
    online journalism, 27
    overview, 21–23
    print media, 26
    television and radio, 26
Multimedia information graphics, *see also South Florida Sun-Sentinel*
    reporters, 87–89
    for single topic, 89–94
Multimedia journalism, *see* media convergence
Multimedia literacy, 153
Multimedia message services (MMS), 173
Multimedia public relations, 185–203
    building relationships, 193
        establishing dialogues, 191–92
        long-term, 192–93
        opting in, 192
        viral communications, 193
        writing skills, 191
    and communities, 200–201
    and employees, 197–200
        blogs, 199
        bulletin or discussion boards, 199–200
        crisis communications, 200
        e-mail, 198–99
        Intranet, 198
        knowledge management, 198
        listservs, 199
        newsletters, 199
    exercises, 203
    and media, 193–97
        accessibility, 195

223

Multimedia public relations
(*continued*)
and media (*continued*)
immediacy, context,
and trust, 194–95
listservs, 194
newsrooms, 196
pitching stories in
e-mails, 195
research and
evaluation, 196
splash pages in crisis
communications, 197
Webcast technology,
197
overview, 185–86
role of Internet in
changing, 185–86
speed of communication,
186
and technological
changes, 186–90
access to top decision
makers, 190
agenda setting, 187
communication
theories, 189
environmental
scanning or awareness,
189–90
ethics and credibility,
188, 190
flexibility, 189
news cycles, 186
research, 189
shift to strategic role,
188
writing and design,
188–89
Multiplier effect, media, 177
Multi-skilled journalists,
152–56
craft mastery and
multimedia literacy,
153
quality of work by,
154–55
visual versus word people,
153–54

N

Names in broadcast writing,
60
Name tab, in FCP, 134
Narrative graphics, 83–84
Narrative structure, 148–49
Natural sound, 62, 119–20
Negroponte, Nicholas, 207
News coverage, 27–30
allocation of resources,
29–30
in blogs, 76–77
breaking news, 30–34
daily editorial meetings,
27–28
storytelling, 28–29
News cycles, 186
News events, importance
of, 7
News filtering and
processing, 210
Newsflow managers, 155
"News Illustrated," 87–89
Newsletters, 199
Newspapers, *see also South
Florida Sun-Sentinel*
Chicago Tribune, 209
editing still photos for,
106
The New York Times, 10
Orlando Sentinel, 14
USA Today, 82
Newsresourcers, 155
Newsrooms, 196
New York Times, The, 10
Nielsen Interactive
Entertainment, 175
Nonlinear editing (NLE),
128–42; *see also* Final
Cut Pro (FCP)
Northrup, Kerry, 7, 154–55
Numbers in broadcast
writing, 56, 59
Nut graphs, 73

O

Online journalism, 27;
see also Explorative
graphics; Instructive
graphics; Narrative

graphics; Simulative
graphics; Writing
editing still photos for,
106–7
information graphics in,
83–85
storytelling in news
coverage, 29
video image composition
for, 119
Openings for stories, 44–45
Opt-in e-mail, *see* listservs
Opting in, 192
Organizational culture, 3–4
Orlando Sentinel, 14
OUT points, in FCP, 133
Overwrite Edit command, in
FCP, 136
Ownership convergence, 4–5

P

Pacing stories on video, 119
Page form for broadcast
writing, 56
Paid search marketing,
170–71
Pans, 118
Papper, Bob, 154
Paul, Nora, 153–54
Pavlik, John, 185–86
Personal Digital Production
(PDP) program,
151–52
Personalized advertising,
see consumer driven
advertising
Photographers, 107–9
and print, video, or
multimedia, 107
safety of while filming
DV, 122
storyboards, 108
throw downs, 108–9
transitional or cutaway
shots, 108
Photojournalism, *see* digital
video (DV); still
photojournalism
Photoshop, 156–57
Pitching stories in e-mails,
195

Platypus journalism, 110
Playback, *see Canvas Window*, in FCP
Presentation or storytelling convergence, 6
Prices, advertising, 168–69
Primacy of information, 157–58
Print media, 15, 26; *see also* Newspapers
  versus broadcast, 153–54
  editing still photos for, 106
  information graphics in, 82
  storytelling in news coverage, 28
Prioritizing information, 43–44
Processing news, 210
Producer-driven stories, 150–51
Producers, 21–36; *see also* Convergence continuum; News coverage
  exercises, 36
  online journalism, 27
  overview, 21–23
  print media, 26
  television and radio, 26
Product placement, 176
Professional television cameras, 115–16
Pronouncers, 58
Pryor, Larry, 4
Public relations, *see* multimedia public relations
Publishing, self, on Web, 69–70

Q

Quotes in Web stories, 73

R

Rack focusing, 118–19
Radio, 26
  and mass media advertising, 166

story formats for, 62, 64–66
  actualities, 62
  live reports or ROSRs, 62
  natural, wild, or ambient sound, 62
  reader, 62, 64
  voicers, 62
  wraparounds, 62
storytelling in news coverage, 28
Radio on scene reports (ROSRs), 62
Razor Blade Tool, in FCP, 138
Readability of broadcast writing, 56–58
  abbreviations, 56
  acronyms and initials, 57
  numbers, 56
  page form, 56
  pronouncers, 58
  sentence length, 57
  sound, 57–58
  symbols, 57
Readers
  radio, 62, 64
  TV, 62–63, 64
Relationships, *see* multimedia public relations
Replace Edit command, in FCP, 136
Reporter-driven stories, 150–51
Reporter packages, 63–64
Reporters, *see also* Multi-skilled journalists; *South Florida Sun-Sentinel*
  graphics, 86–89
  and multimedia, 87–89
  precision of, 86
  Web, 77–78
Reporting, 41–43
  background, 41–42
  depth of, 42–43
  gathering extra information, 42
  interviews, 42
  news in blogs, 76

Reports, live, 62, 63–64
Research in public relations, 189, 196
Resource allocation in news coverage, 29–30
Retail media networks, 176
Rosenblum, Michael, 151–52

S

Safety, photographer, 122
Schools, journalism, 16–17
Scratch Disks setting of FCP, 130–31
Search engine marketing, 170–71
Self-publishing on Web, 69–70
Sentences in broadcast writing
  length of, 57
  simplicity of, 60–61
Sequences, 118–19
  in FCP, 134–35
  Linking and *Snapping* indicators, 135
  Name tab, 134
  Timeline, 134–35
Setup and storage, FCP, 129–31
  Autosave Vault setting, 131
  Easy Setup dialog, 131
  Scratch Disks setting, 130–31
  System Settings dialog, 130–31
Sharing content, 24–25
Shooting DV, *see* digital video (DV)
Short message services (SMS), 173
Shotgun microphones, 120
Shovelware, 71
Shuttle Control, in FCP, 137
Simulative graphics, 83–85
Singapore Press Holdings (SPH), 10–11
Slideshow editing, 106–7
Smith, W. Eugene, 109
Snapping indicators, in FCP, 135

Soft-sell advertising, 167
Sound, *see also* Audio for
 digital video
 in broadcast writing,
  57–58
 natural, wild, or ambient,
  in radio, 62
Sound on tape (SOT), 63
Sources, attribution of, 60
South Florida Sun-Sentinel,
 87–90
 explorative graphics, 85
 graphics director Don
  Wittekind, 89
 instructive graphics, 84
 "News Illustrated," 87–89
 simulative graphics, 85
 Spiegel Grove project,
  91–94
 "The Edge," 89–90
Special-interest blogs, 77
Speech and writing for
 broadcast, 55–67; *see
  also* Story formats
 exercises, 67
 overview, 55–56
 rules for readability,
  56–58
  abbreviations, 56
  acronyms and initials,
   57
  numbers, 56
  page form, 56
  pronouncers, 58
  sentence length, 57
  sound, 57–58
  symbols, 57
 understandability rules,
  58–62
  attribution before
   statements, 60
  chronological story
   development, 61–62
  contractions, 59–60
  informality, 58–59
  leads, 61
  numbers, 59
  sentence simplicity,
   60–61
  titles before names, 60

 voice and tense, 61
 word choice, 59
Speed of communication,
 186
Spiegel Grove project, 91–94
Spillman, Mary, 5, 24
Splash pages, 197
steadiness of digital video,
 121–22
Stevens, Jane, 150–51
Stick microphones, 120
Still photojournalism,
 99–112
 democratization of,
  102–4
 digital, 104–5
 editing, 105–7
  Burns's documentary
   techniques, 106–7
  interactivity, 107
  newspapers and
   magazines, 106
  Web, video, TV, and
   slideshow, 106–7
 ethics and truth in, 109
 exercises, 112
 and multimedia, 100,
  110–11
 overview, 99
 photographer
  responsibilities, 107–9
  in print, video, or
   multimedia, 107
  storyboards, 108
  throw downs, 108–9
  transitional or
   cutaway shots, 108
 and technology, 100–102,
  104
Stone, Martha, 149, 154
Storage, FCP, *see* setup and
 storage, FCP
Storyboards, 108
Storybuilders, 155
Story formats, 62–66; *see also*
 Readers
 for radio, 62, 64–66
  actualities, 62
  live reports or ROSRs,
   62

  natural, wild, or
   ambient sound, 62
  voicers, 62
  wraparounds, 62
 for television, 62–66
  double boxes, 63–64
  live reports, 63–64
  reporter packages,
   63–64
  voiceover and sound
   on tape, 63
Storytelling, 28–29
 chronological, in
  broadcast, 61–62
 in digital video, 121–22
 and media convergence,
  148–49
 for multimedia
  photography, 111
 online, 29
 or presentation
  convergence, 6
 in print, 28
 radio, 28
 on television, 28–29
Strategic role of public
 relations, 188
Structural convergence, 5–6
Structure, for writing, *see*
 writing
Sulzberger, Arthur O., Jr.,
 9–10
*Sun-Sentinel, South Florida,
 see South Florida
 Sun-Sentinel*
Superimpose Edit command,
 in FCP, 137
Symbols in broadcast writing,
 57
System Settings dialog of FCP,
 130–31

T

Tactical convergence, 5
Tape, sound on, (SOT), 63
Telegraph, 205–6
Television, 26; *see also*
 Interactive TV (iTV)
 editing still photos for,
  106–7

and mass media
 advertising
  broadcast versus cable,
   167–69
  hard-sell and soft-sell
   techniques, 167
 professional cameras,
  115–16
 readers, 62–64
 story formats for, 62–66
  double boxes, 63–64
  live reports, 63–64
  reporter packages,
   63–64
  voiceover and sound
   on tape, 63
 storytelling in news
  coverage, 28–29
Tense in broadcast, 61
Text-messaging, 173
Text use on Web, 70–71
"The Edge," 89–90
Thelen, Gil, 153
Thesis statements, 123
Throw downs, 108–9
Timeline, in FCP, 134–35,
 137
Timing of stories on video,
 119
Titles in broadcast writing, 60
Toolbar, in FCP, 138
Tools for convergent
 journalists, 158
Track Select Tool, in FCP, 138
Training convergence
 journalists, 149
Transitional shots, 108
Trends, media, 12–13
Tripods, 121–22
Trust, 194–95
Truth in photographs, 109
Tyner, Howard, 8, 152–53

U

Understandability of
 broadcast writing,
 58–62
 attribution before
  statements, 60

chronological story
 development, 61–62
 contractions, 59–60
 informality, 58–59
 leads, 61
 numbers, 59
 sentence simplicity,
  60–61
 titles before names, 60
 voice and tense, 61
 word choice, 59
Universities, 16–17
USA Today, 82

V

Video editing, 106–7; *see also*
 Digital video (DV)
Video games, 174–75
 advergaming, 174
 dynamic in-game, 174
 in-game ads, 174
 measuring ad exposure,
  175
Video Journalist (VJ)
 program, 151–52
Viewer Window, in FCP,
 137–38
Viral communications, 193
Voice in broadcast, 61
Voiceovers (VO), 63
Voicers, 62
VTR controls, in FCP, 132,
 137

W

Web-based journalism, *see*
 online journalism;
 writing
Webcams, 172
Webcast technology, 197
Web logs, *see* blogs
White and black balancing,
 116–17, 129
Wild sound, 62, 119–20
Wireless microphones,
 120–21
Wittekind, Don, 89
Word choice in broadcast
 writing, 59

Worldwide media
 convergence, 12–13
Wraparounds, 62
Writers
 as editors, 47–48
 for Web, 77–78
Writing, 39–52; *see also*
  Blogs; Inverted
  pyramid method;
  Speech and writing for
  broadcast
 basic structure, 44–47
  closure, 45
  details, 46
  middle material,
   46–47
  openings, 44–45
 and editing, 47–50
  as collaborative
   process, 48–49
  final edit, 49–50
  versus fixing copy,
   48–49
  by writer, 47–48
 exercises, 52
 and multimedia public
  relations, 188–89, 191
 as necessary skill for
  convergence, 40–41,
  211
 overview, 39–40
 and reporting, 41–43
  background, 41–42
  depth of, 42–43
  gathering extra
   information, 42
  interviews, 42
 for Web, 69–79
  challenge of, 77–78
  interactivity, 70
  and multimedia, 70,
   74–75
  overview, 69–70
  self-publishing, 69–70
  writers and reporters,
   77–78

Z

Zooms, 118
Zoom Tool, in FCP, 138